THE REDEMPTION STORY

WERNER TRAPP

THE REDEMPTION STORY

Copyright © 2010 Werner Trapp

All rights reserved. No part of this publication may be reproduced, stored in a retrieval system, or transmitted in any form or by any means—electronic, mechanical, photocopy, recording, or any other—except for brief quotations in printed reviews, without prior permission from the publisher.

Unless otherwise indicated, all scripture quotations are taken from the New King James Version/Thomas Nelson Publishers, Nashville: Thomas Nelson Publishers, Copyright © 1984. Used by permission. All rights reserved.

Scripture quotations marked AMP are taken from The Amplified Bible Old Testament, Copyright © 1965, 1987 by the Zondervan Corporation and The Amplified New Testament, Copyright © 1958, 1987 by The Lockman Foundation. Used by permission. All rights reserved.

ISBN-13: 978-1-77069-132-2

Word Alive Press
131 Cordite Road, Winnipeg, MB R3W 1S1
www.wordalivepress.ca

Library and Archives Canada Cataloguing in Publication

Trapp, Werner, 1926-
    The redemption story / Werner Trapp.

Includes bibliographical references.
ISBN 978-1-77069-132-2

    1. Theology, Doctrinal--Popular works. 2. Theology, Doctrinal--Miscellanea. 3. Evangelicalism--Miscellanea. I. Title.

BT77.T73 2010   230'.04624   C2010-907242-1

This book is dedicated to the memory of
Mr. August Ellenberg, Secretary of the Evangelical
Young Men's Society, Fritzlar chapter,
in Hesse, Germany.

He was the first person who
led me into Christian ministry.

"Therefore every scribe instructed concerning the kingdom of heaven is like a householder who brings out of his treasure things new and old."
—**Jesus Christ**
(**Matthew** 13:52)

WORDS OF APPRECIATION

I wish to offer my heartfelt thanks to my dear wife Helen for bearing with me during the time I processed this book.

I thank my son Eberhardt for all his kind and tireless help with the computer work, and my son Harold and Mr. Benno Klaassen, B.A. for their reviews of this book and enthusiastic support to publish it.

Special mention goes to my editor, Evan Braun of Word Alive Press, for his critique, patience, and late night work to get this book ready for publication.

May our Lord Jesus Christ bless you all for your encouragements.

A brother in Jesus,

—Rev. Werner Trapp, BBR

This book is neither a perfect nor an exhaustive presentation of its subject matter. Rather, it is a short presentation of topics the author feels are necessary to make the point for important issues that religious and non-religious people may have concerning the Neo-Evangelical insights and outlook on age-old beliefs and hopes of the Christian faith. This book is written to engender interest in spiritual and religious matters, and for people to become better acquainted with the Bible and Church history in a compact way.

Some readers may be sceptical about the term "Neo-Evangelicals." This is a group of Christians whose faith is based on four absolutes, or pillars of faith: the Bible, True Science, True History, and Common Sense. May this book be a blessing to the reader.

TABLE OF CONTENTS

Introduction		xiii
1.	What Are Some of These Evidences?	1
2.	Things that Prove God's Existence to Me	4
3.	The Role of God in the World's Religions	7
4.	The Development of the God Idea	8
5.	Thoughts About the Message of the Bible	11
6.	The Creations God Accomplished through Jesus Christ	15
7.	There Are Five Creations Written About in the Bible	16
8.	The Cause of the Destruction of the First Creation	20

9.	God's Redemptive Work Begins	23
10.	The High Points of This Struggle Between God and Satan	27
11.	A New Beginning	30
12.	The Great Confusion	33
13.	Abraham, the Man of Faith	36
14.	God's Plan of Redemption Continued	42
15.	Joseph, God's Man of Action	43
16.	Pharaoh's Dreams	45
17.	The Man God Used to Bring Liberty to Israel	48
18.	Moses' Spiritual Awakening	49
19.	The Deliverer at Work	51
20.	How Did Israel Do It?	56
21.	The Important Events that Impact Us Living Today	61
22.	Israel's Disobedience	65
23.	Particulars of Prophecies Regarding the Son of God, the Saviour Jesus Christ	69
24.	A Compact Presentation of Christ's Ministry on Earth	72
25.	Some of the Teachings of Jesus	74
26.	Conflict with Israel's Leaders	76
27.	The Conflict Issues	79
28.	The Passion of Jesus Christ	81
29.	The Resurrection of Jesus Christ	84
30.	How the Christian Church Came to Be	91
31.	The Happenings at the Feast of Pentecost	94
32.	Things that Happened After Pentecost	97
33.	The Progress of the Early Church	101
34.	The Church Under the Apostolic Fathers	104

35.	The Rise of the Roman Catholic Church	108
36.	The Evangelical Revivals (1170 A.D.—Present)	112
37.	A Short History of the Pentecostal/Charismatic Revivals	114
38.	Signs that the Return of Our Lord Jesus Is Near at Hand	118
39.	The Conflict of the "Great Tribulation" Is Imprinted in the Geographical Shapes of Europe	126
40.	What Will Happen After the Defeat of Anti-Christ and Satan at Armageddon?	130
41.	Things that Happen After the Rapture	133
42.	What Will Happen in Israel Right After the Return of the Lord Jesus Christ?	136
43.	The Great Judgement Day at the Great White Throne	139
44.	Where Is Heaven Now, and What Can We Find in It?	141

Bibliography 147

INTRODUCTION

From my childhood days forward, my dad wanted to make me an atheist like himself. However, I could never see any sense in this belief, because to me nothing can come out of nothing. To me, there had to be a first cause of everything, and that cause was God. What confirmed me in my belief was what my mom told me about God. She was a Christian.

During my eighty-four years of life, my belief has often been challenged. First in high school in Germany, and then later through various claims of atheistic naturalistic scientists. Their basic premise is the Darwinian Theory of Evolution. But increasingly in our days, more and more scientists have come to reject that theory, and even some evolutionists now admit that life on earth did not evolve gradually as formerly believed, but that different life forms appeared on earth suddenly. Now, there are only two possibilities for how such a thing could happen: either they came from outer space, or else an intelligent being like God created them here.

A growing group of scientists have come to believe in Intelligent Design. They have discovered proofs of this. The Apostle Paul says in his letter to the Romans, *"For that which is known about God is evident to [people] and made plain in their inner consciousness, because God Himself has shown it to them. For ever since the creation of the world His invisible nature and attributes, that is, His eternal power and divinity, have been made intelligible and clearly discernible in and through the things that have been made (His handiworks). So men are without excuse [not to trust Him]"* (Romans 1:19–20, AMP).

I will now quote some information coming from Lee Strobel's book, *The Case For A Creator*. I strongly recommend it. He provides some very good answers for us.

Stephen C. Meyer, Doctor of Philosophy, is a professor at Witworth College and a senior fellow at the Centre for Science and Culture at the Discovery Institute in Seattle. He says: "Scientific evidence actually supports theistic belief (belief in God as Creator and Sustainer). In fact, across a wide range of the sciences, evidence has come to light in the last fifty years which, taken together, provides a robust case for theism. Only theism can provide an intellectually satisfying causal explanation for all this evidence."[1]

---

[1] Strobel, Lee. *The Case for a Creator*. Grand Rapids, MI: Zondervan (2004), p. 89.

1.
WHAT ARE SOME OF THESE EVIDENCES?

Evidence from Cosmology: William Lane Craig is a Doctor of Philosophy and Theology at the Talbot School of Theology. He is a member of nine professional societies, including the American Philosophical Association, the Science and Religion Forum, the American Scientific Affiliation, and the Philosophy of Time Society. He says: "In atheism the universe just pops into being out of nothing, with absolutely no explanation at all. I think once people understand the concept of absolute nothingness, it's simply obvious to them that if something has a beginning, that it could not have popped into being out of nothing but must have a cause that brings it into existence..."[2] The universe's age must be finite—that is, it must have had a beginning. "Predictions about the 'Big Bang' (the starting point of the universe) have been consistently verified by scientific data."[3]

Evidence of Physics: Robin Collins is a Professor Doctor of Philosophy, Postdoctoral fellow at Northwestern University, long-time researcher, writer, and teacher at Messiah College. He says: "In physics we see an uncanny

---
[2] Ibid. p. 121.
[3] Ibid. p. 129.

degree of harmony, symmetry and proportionality. And we see something that I call 'discoverability.' By that I mean that the laws of nature seem to have been carefully arranged so that they can be discovered by beings of our level of intelligence. That not only fits the idea of design (by God), but it also suggests a providential purpose for humankind—that is to learn about our habitat and to develop science and technology."[4] Again this points to a creator, God.

Patrick Glynn, a former famous atheist, says: "The entropic evidence... does offer as strong an indication as reason and science alone could be expected to provide that God exists... Ironically, the picture of the universe bequeathed to us by the most advanced twentieth century science is closer in spirit to the vision presented in the Book of Genesis (the first book of the Bible) than anything offered by science since Copernicus."[5]

Evidence of Astronomy: Jay Wesley Richards is an academic overachiever. He holds three advanced degrees in philosophy and theology, including a doctorate from Princeton Theological Seminary.[6] He quotes a colleague, O'Keefe, as saying: "We are, by astronomical standards, a pampered, cosseted, cherished group of creatures; our Darwinian claim to have done it all ourselves is as ridiculous and as charming as a baby's brave effort to stand on its own feet and refuse its mother's hand. If the universe had not been made with the most exacting precision we could never have come into existence. It is my view that these circum-

---

[4] Ibid. p. 181.
[5] Ibid. p. 185.
[6] Ibid. p. 197.

The Redemption Story

stances indicate the universe was created for man to live in."[7]

There are furthermore amazing evidences of God as our creator in the sciences of biochemistry, biology, and consciousness by equally qualified persons. Let me paraphrase this article from an issue of Reader's Digest of many years ago: When our astronomers viewed the heavens through modern telescopes etc. they discovered that the whole universe looks like sand on a beach for a lot of celestial bodies except for one place: In the north. Beyond the north star, they discovered the only dark hole in all the lights of heaven. This hole was bordered by such a mass of heavenly bodies, shaped like a pear or a church bell, and exerting such a tremendous glory, that the viewers were overcome by a strong feeling of awe, saying, if there is indeed a God, then that must be His abode.

Interestingly, the Bible confirms the same things in the Book of Job (1500 BC): *"[God] stretches out the north over empty space"* (Job 26:7). It is also confirmed in the Book of Isaiah (700 BC): *"And you [Satan] have said in your heart, I will ascend to heaven; I will exalt my throne above the stars of God; I will sit upon the mount of assembly in the uttermost north. I will ascend above the heights of the clouds; I will make myself like the Most High [God]"* (Isaiah 13:13–14).

---

[7] Ibid. p. 237.

2.

THINGS THAT PROVE GOD'S EXISTENCE TO ME

1. First, there is the miracle of my birth. My mother had an accident causing me to be born two months premature. She was in the process of bleeding to death, and I was born a "blue baby," not responding to life. The physician laid me on a table, not expecting me to live, and worked on stopping my mother's bleedings. After two hours, a nurse asked the doctor what to do with me. He looked at me and said, "Let's give it one more try," so they went back to work on me and I finally responded. According to present scientific knowledge, I should be severely brain damaged due to a lack of oxygen to the brain for such a prolonged period. But I turned out normal, praise God!

2. I suffered from an ear infection for one year between the ages of three and four. There were no antibiotics available at that time that could help me. One Wednesday, a midget man talked to my mother about my condition and told her to place one small onion against each ear, cut to let fumes escape into the ear. She prayed that it would work, since I was due for surgery on Friday of the same week. When the physician checked my ears, however, both ears were fine.

The Redemption Story

3. In 1933, our family became political refugees, fleeing to Sweden from Nazi Germany. I became a foster child in the home of one of the Swedish national government's elected officials. His family had a hobby garden across the river with some chickens, which I went to feed on Saturdays. One Saturday, while there was still thick ice on the river, I didn't notice that the ice breaker had already gone by and I happened to slide onto small broken ice fragments. I could not return to the solid ice, because the ice sunk down under my own weight. I grew very scared and called upon my Father in heaven to save me, and He brought me across the shipping lane where big ships went by. I didn't so much as get water in my boots. I should have drowned, a civil engineer once told me. He claimed that only a miracle of God had saved my life. After the accident, I walked back home over a bridge not far away. Because of this experience, I have no problems believing the story in the New Testament of Jesus walking on the Sea of Galilee.

4. On my eleventh birthday, I had a dream of judgment day that shocked me.

5. God saved my life at least ten times during the Battle of Berlin in April 1945 when Russian soldiers shot at me with rifle bullets, cannon shells, and threw hand grenades. I was not hurt.

6. When I was about twenty years old (in 1946), Jesus revealed Himself in my life and forgave me my sins. I became spiritually born again. Ever since that day, I have been a Christian and follower of Jesus Christ.

7. God called my name three times one night in 1955. The voice was so very loud that I woke up from my midnight sleep and answered Him. I was shocked. He told me to do something which I did not want to do, and I couldn't fall back asleep until sunrise, when I gave in to God's demands and answered, "Yes."

8. God poured His Spirit out on me one Sunday night in church in November 1963 in a very powerful way. He equipped me with some spiritual gifts.

9. I had a dream in 1963, which God explained to me two years later in great detail. No pastor or church elder had ever been able to explain it to me. It is in part because of God's interpretation of that dream that I went to Bible school and became a pastor. I completed my studies with a Bachelor of Bible Research degree.

10. On June 28, 1998, I passed out during a morning church service. My family and I thought I was going to die, but instead God simply took me to heaven for a few minutes. It was so beautiful there—I cannot fully explain to anyone just how beautiful heaven is, because there are no human words available to do it justice. I did not want to come back, but God sent me back anyway. That is why I am here today.

These are some of my life's experiences that prove God's existence to me. It would not make any difference what an atheist scientist could say against it, because I have experienced these things, and nobody can take them away from me.

3.
THE ROLE OF GOD IN THE WORLD'S RELIGIONS

There are many religions in the world that want to worship a deity, or many gods, that they believe exist. There are the Moslems who believe Allah to be the only god in the universe. History tells that Mohammed learned more about the one and only God from Jewish refugees living in Arabia. They spoke of Him as "Eloah" which in Arabic is "Allah."[8] Then there is Hinduism, which believes in millions of gods, both good and evil. Then comes Buddhism, which follows the teachings of Buddha. This faith is actually not a religion in its proper sense, but rather a philosophy of life, since Buddha never claimed to have knowledge of a personal god. He was merely a good prince who came to have a rather pessimistic view of life by observing the fates of a lot of people. Because of this, he sought out a way to eliminate the extreme emotions of sadness and happiness, because these emotions caused problems to many people. His hope was to arrive at nirvana, a state where the individual existence is supposed to be dissolved into an existing supreme spirit. This he considered the highest state of blessedness.

---

[8] Zierer, Otto. *Weltgeschichte, Volume 29*. Murnau, Germany: Sebastian Lux Verlag, p. 202.

At one time, there was some form of ancestor worship all over the world. It still exists in parts of Africa and Asia. Some forms of this belief lead to the acceptance of many gods.

Then follows the religion of Animism. According to this religion, gods and/or spirits can be found in any natural object like an animal, plant, or mineral (such as a stone, for example). This religion is found mainly in Africa, though it also can be found in some places in Asia and America. Many American natives believe in a creator spirit. An important branch of Animism is the ancient religion of Wicca. Wiccans believe in witches and warlocks, Mother Earth, etc. The modern "New Age" religion adopts many of its ideas.

However, the true and living God revealed Himself to Adam, the first Middle East man.

4.

THE DEVELOPMENT OF THE GOD IDEA

The reports concerning this God come from Adam and some of his descendants. These people came to be called "Hebrews." The experiences they had with God were collected and published by a Hebrew prince named Moses. To him the Five Books of Moses are credited. These are: Genesis, Exodus, Leviticus, Numbers, and Deuteronomy—

The Redemption Story

the first five books in the Bible. They are considered to be inspired by God.

Further inspired writings were added by the Hebrew people that came after him. They were collected under God's supervision until they were completed within a time frame of 1,600 years, from 1500 B.C. to 100 A.D. This collection of holy books is called the Bible, which simply means "The Book."

Though the authors of most of these books descended from a man called "Eber" or "Heber," the name of their nationality changed through the ages. Over time, they came to be known as Israelites. Later, they were called Jews. The Jews who returned to their ancient homeland in 1948 (to the land of Canaan, or Palestine) re-established their nation under the banner of Israel, in accord with the ancient prophesies in the Bible. They are now called Israelis. They are brothers of the Arabs.

In the Bible, God is revealed as being the only existing God, who is the Creator and Sustainer of everything in the universe. He is a benevolent God of a pure and holy character who cares about His creation. Therefore, He is called "the God of Love," because He does everything out of love—even severe punishments when they must be applied to people. He is omniscient (all-knowing), omnipresent (all-present), and omnipotent (all-powerful). He also has a name. That name, in Hebrew, is "Yahweh," meaning "The Eternally Existing One." In 1415 A.D., someone combined the name Yahweh with the vowels of the Hebrew language word for "Lord," which is "Adonai," and came up with the name "Jehovah."

In my view, He cannot be the God of Love unless He has somebody to give His love to. Yes, one can and should love oneself, but ordinarily a person has a need to express his or her love upon someone else. So it is also with God.

Throughout the Bible, we discover that God always existed in three personalities: the first is called "the Father," the second "the Son," and the third "the Holy Spirit." Most Christians speak therefore of "one God in three persons." or "the Holy Trinity, Three in One," which is also called the Godhead.

Through my studies, I have come to the conclusion that the Godhead is a family. In the biblical languages, the Father is addressed in masculine terms, the Holy Spirit in feminine terms, and the Son again in masculine terms. That looks like a family to me. Most Christians also believe that the Godhead is a Spirit, and they claim that a spirit has no body. I like to differ. In the first book of the Bible, the first chapter of Genesis, God created mankind "according to His likeness," or in the image of God. The Hebrew words in question are *demuwth* and *Tselem*. These two words imply first of all a physical likeness, more so than a likeness in intelligence, conscience etc. Therefore I say that we are a likeness of the Godhead in spirit, soul, and body. The Father, the Holy Spirit, and the Son have bodies that resemble ours, except that they are made up of a spiritual material, while we are made of a physical material.

The difference is explained in the New Testament (see 1 Corinthians 15:35–49). In contrast to us, spirits have the ability to unite themselves as many into one, or vice versa, according to the Gospel story of Luke (see Luke 8:26–30).

This is why the spirits in that story used the personal pronouns of both "I" and "we" at the same time. To spirits, physical size is also very relative. God can fill the universe with Himself. In the biblical books of Ezekiel and Daniel, spirits are called "angels," who appeared as giants in size and were always masculine. Spirits can also be so small that they can hide in bacteria and viruses and cause sickness among people. The reason for this is that there are good and evil spirits. I will write about them a bit more later in this book.

5.
THOUGHTS ABOUT THE MESSAGE OF THE BIBLE

The theme of the entire book can be said to be: "God's redemptive work for humanity's happiness." It consist of two "Testaments," the Old Testament and the New Testament. The Old Testament's theme is: "God's preparations for mankind's redemption." The New Testament's theme is: "God's finished work for mankind's redemption." The word "Testament" implies the last will of a person, to be applied after his or her death. In the Bible, God's Son, Jesus Christ, died for the sins of mankind so that we could regain an eternal life of happiness according to His will.

All people have fallen away from God and therefore deserve punishment. We are all born "godless," not knowing anything about God, nor caring about God. The Apostle Paul writes to the Roman Church the following: *"For all have sinned and fall short of the glory of God, being justified freely by His grace through the redemption that is in Christ Jesus"* (Romans 3:23–24). In the book of Acts, Doctor Luke writes, *"Nor is there salvation in any other, for there is no other name under heaven given among men by which we must be saved [for our eternal happiness]"* (Acts 4:12).

Why is that so? You see, the Son of God was given a human body through His birth into this world by the virgin Mary, when God's time schedule was fulfilled for that purpose (Galatians 4:4). He received the name Jesus, meaning "Saviour." He is actually the Creator of everything by the Father's authority. When mankind fell away from God, it did damage to the owner, God the Father. Since mankind was created by Jesus, He bears the responsibility for this damage in the same manner that a dog's owner has to pay for the damage his dog inflicts on a neighbour. Jesus, as the Creator of all of us, had to bear the punishment on our behalf so that we could be set free from sin. He accomplished this through His death on the cross.

But He did not stay in death. As the Son of the living God, He has life in Himself just like His Father has, according to John 5:26. Therefore He rose from the dead, because He had this power in Himself, and was witnessed alive after His resurrection. He touched people and was seen and heard by more than five hundred people at once next to the Apostles and various women. He then went on to His

The Redemption Story

heavenly home and now represents us to His Father, just as a lawyer speaks for his clients before a judge. Therefore the words that Jesus Himself spoke in the Gospel of John are believable and true: *"For God so loved the world [mankind] that He gave His only begotten Son, that whoever believes in [trusts in, clings to, and relies on] Him should not perish [come to destruction, be lost] but have [possess in the present] everlasting life"* (John 3:16).

Right now, this eternal life lives in the followers of Jesus Christ. True, our fleshly body must still die. It is only a "tent" in which the real You now lives. At death, this real You will go to heaven to be with Jesus and the Father until resurrection day, provided that we have accepted Jesus Christ as our Saviour and Lord and follow His teaching. Then we will be given a body like God has and experience death, pain, and sorrow no more. We will then be fully completed members of God's family. What a beautiful faith this is, right?

Now a few more words about the Bible. All the thousands of ancient writings that still exist today, except perhaps for the Book of Isaiah (700 BC), are copies, because the originals have worn out of existence. Because there exist thousands of copies, we can determine through the sciences of papyrology and archaeology what the original scriptures actually said. The copies contain mistakes which are easily recognizable. These do not interfere with the true teachings of the Bible in the least. However, Evangelicals believe that every word of the original Bible has been inspired by God. This is an act of faith. Evidentially, we cannot prove this. So far, we can speak honestly only of an "inspired content."

Any word found in the Bible is there, because God purposed it to be there... even the mistakes.

It becomes very clear when, for example, comparing the writings of the Prophet Isaiah, who was a well-educated statesman, and the writings of the Prophet Amos, who was only a shepherd. Isaiah's writings have very few spelling mistakes, while Amos has some, owing to the fact that he was not so well-educated. However, his message is nevertheless highly inspired by God. It is as the Apostle Paul says in 2 Corinthians 4:7, *"But we have this treasure [the Word of God] in earthen vessels, that the excellence of the power may be of God and not of us."* Psalm 119:160 says, *"The sum of Your Word is truth [the total of the full meaning of all Your individual precepts]"* (AMP).

Let's take a moment to look at the organisation of the Bible.

The Old Testament has seventeen books of history, five books of wisdom literature, and seventeen books of the Prophets. The New Testament has five books of history, twenty-one books of teaching, and one prophetical book, "The Revelation of Jesus Christ." The Bible contains a total of forty-seven books of prophetic teaching, partly telling of future happenings, of which it is alleged that 80% has already been fulfilled. This proves that its origin is from the living God, unlike any other religious book in the world. By a good reader, the Bible can be read through in seventy-six hours. Not so bad!

6.

THE CREATIONS GOD ACCOMPLISHED THROUGH JESUS CHRIST

The Bible says in Genesis 1:1, *"In the beginning God created the heavens [plural] and the earth."* So it reads in the English translations of the Bible. In the original Hebrew, there is no word for "God." The Hebrew term which is translated "God" is actually "Elohim," which means "the Almighty Ones." This plural is a confirmation of something I alluded to earlier, that the Godhead created the world through the Son.

In English, some Bible verses confirm this. For example, the Gospel of John 1:3 says, *"All things were made through Him [Jesus, the Son of God]."* Then, a few verses later: *"He was in the world, and the world was made through Him"* (John 1:10). The Apostle Paul's letter to the Colossians says: *"For by Him all things were created that are in heaven and that are on earth"* (Colossians 1:16). Finally, in the letter to the Hebrews, it says, *"God, who at various times and in various ways spoke in time past to the fathers by the prophets, has in these last days spoken to us by His Son, whom He has appointed heir of all things, through whom also He made the worlds"* (Hebrews 1:1–2).

So the situation is clear. In Genesis 1, the Almighty Ones (Father, Son, and the Holy Spirit) were all actively involved in creation.

7.

THERE ARE FIVE CREATIONS WRITTEN ABOUT IN THE BIBLE

1. Genesis 1:1 is the first creation. When did it take place? Some Evangelicals believe it happened six thousand years ago, because the genealogies of the Old Testament begin at that time. It must be admitted that, according to Genesis 1, God created things in sudden steps over a period of time. This probably happened between six billion and twenty billion years ago according to trustworthy scientists. Why is there such a large gap of uncertainty? Because the farther back science tries to trace history, the more difficult it becomes. Astronomy shows that things began with a "Big Bang," and science is unable to learn anything beyond that point in space and time. We say humorously, "God said BANG! and everything came about."

The Redemption Story 17

The Bible says that God created things "out of nothing." The Bible explains what this "nothing" is in the Letter to the Hebrews: *"By faith we understand that the worlds were framed by the word of God, so that the things which are <u>seen were not made of things which are visible</u>"* (Hebrews 11:3, emphasis mine). There are a lot of "invisible things" around: air, other gases, certain solar rays, etc., so there we have no problem accepting Biblical statements.

2. From Genesis 1:2 to Genesis 2:4, we are given an account of the second creation. A second creation was necessary, since the first creation was destroyed, as shown in Genesis 1:2, where the Hebrew words *"tohu va bohu"* actually mean "made waste and destroyed."[9] In Isaiah 45:18, it says, *"[God] formed the earth and made it... formed it to be inhabited: [saying] 'I am the Lord, and there is no other.'"* So this first creation had life, but it perished. Why? I will deal with this question later. The second creation ends by giving us the name of the Creator: Yahweh, transliterated into English as "LORD."[10]

The last creative act of God in this creation was to create people. He created them in His image. I explained what that encompasses earlier in "The Development of the God

---

[9] Dake, Finis Jennings. *Dake's Annotated Reference Bible*. Atlanta: Dake Bible Sales (1963), p. 1, note m. Also: Scofield, C.I. *The Scofield Reference Bible*. New York: Oxford University Press (1945), p. 3, note 3.

[10] Why is this name of God transliterated as "LORD" in most English Bibles? Not because of an evil intent to hide God's true name, but out of respect for this holy and awesome name. We have inherited this attitude from our Jewish ancestors, who never to this day speak out the name of God as "Yahweh" or "Jehovah." Wherever this name of God is found written in the Old Testament, the Jewish person rendered it with the pronoun "He," or with "the Almighty," or any other word descriptive of God. We follow their example.

Idea." This creation began in Africa, with the creation of the Negroid form of mankind. Out of it developed the Mongoloid form of mankind. This happened about fifty thousand years ago.[11] This explanation does not imply an acceptance of Darwinian evolution.

3. Genesis 2:5–7 and 21–22 tells us of the third creation. Out of it came the Adamite people, which developed later into the Japhetites (Caucasians), Semites (Jews and Arabs), and the Hamites (Ethiopians and Cushites). This indeed took place about six thousand years ago. They populated the Middle East, North Africa, and Europe. In contrast to the previous creations of mankind, the Adamite peoples are distinguished from the others not necessarily by skin colour, but by facial features (longer faces, narrow lips, slender cheeks, little or no valley from the forehead to the nose and sometimes eagle beak noses), body hair mass, and hair colour (including light blond, prevalent among Scandinavians).

4. The fourth creation refers to the creation of the "new man." It is presently still ongoing. The "new man" creation refers to the transformation of anyone from any human race, according to Paul's letter to the Galatians: *"For in Christ Jesus neither circumcision nor uncircumcision avails anything, but a new creation"* (Galatians 6:15). Paul's Letter to the Ephesians says: *"That you put on the <u>new man</u> which was created according to God, in true righteousness and holiness"* (Ephesians 4:24, emphasis mine). What this really means is a transformation of the natural man, complete with his sinfulness and worldly attitude, into a new spiritual creation. As Paul expresses it in

---

[11] *Encyclopaedia Britannica, Book 14,* 1967, p. 737d.

his second letter to the Corinthians, *"If anyone is in Christ [that is, has accepted Jesus Christ as his/her personal Saviour and Lord and obeys His teaching], he is a new creation; old things have passed away; behold, all things [in that person, attitudes, feelings and conscience] have become new"* (2 Corinthians 5:17).

5. The fifth creation will take place after this old world has come to its final end. The resurrection of all peoples will have taken place by this time, as well as the judgment of everybody before God. The Apostle John speaks of it in the book of Revelation, the last book in the Bible. He says: *"I saw a new heaven and a new earth, for the first heaven and the first earth had passed away"* (Revelation 21:1). God will be seen by His people and be in their midst. *"God will wipe away every tear from their eyes; there shall be no more death, nor sorrow, nor crying. There shall be no more pain, for the former things have passed away... But the cowardly, unbelieving, abominable, murderers, sexually immoral, sorcerers [illicit drug users], idolators, and all liars shall have their part in the lake which burns with fire and brimstone"* (Revelation 21:4,8). This is eternity.

8.
THE CAUSE OF THE DESTRUCTION OF THE FIRST CREATION

The first creation was destroyed by Satan in his rebellion against God. Who is Satan? Many people and some scientists believe that there is life somewhere else in the universe, and they have even given us a number of theories and fantasies about these possibilities. In the early 1900s, stories were told of Martians coming from the planet Mars to conquer Earth. We now know that nobody can live on Mars. In the 1930s, my grandma gave me a book called *The Flight to Venus*, in which a space flight crew landed on Venus in their space ship, and oh what a paradise it was! The reality is that Venus is extremely hot. And so people went on up to the little green men of our time, the "aliens from outer space" that come out of "flying saucers."

The Bible tells us that there is life in the universe. It mentions angels, seraphim, and cherubim. In the letter to the Colossian church, the Apostle Paul speaks of *"visible and invisible... thrones or dominions or principalities or powers"* (Colossians 1:16). They are also called "sons of God" (in Job 1:6, for example) and the "morning stars" of heaven (Job

38:7). There exist at least one hundred million of them in the universe (Revelation 5:11). Jude, the half-brother of Jesus, speaks of *"angels who did not keep their proper domain, but left their own abode"* (Jude 6).

The order of beings in the universe is as follows:

1. Cherubim
2. Seraphim
3. Angels

Cherubim are angelic princes. Two are named in the Bible: Gabriel, the messenger of the Holy Spirit (Daniel 9:21 and Luke 1:26), and Michael, the angel prince responsible for Israel, one of the angelic chief princes (Daniel 10:13).

Satan was the highest and mightiest angelic prince, next to God. He is called a "cherub" (cherubim is plural). He had a throne in heaven. His former name was Lucifer, meaning "Son of the rising light." In the ancient past, he became full of pride and jealousy. He rebelled against God. He wanted to topple God from His throne and claim it for himself. The Prophet Isaiah tells the story in his book (Isaiah 14:12–15). Lucifer was the steward of the earth in the name of God, according to Luke 4:6. He was thrown out of God's heaven. Jesus said that He *"saw Satan fall like lightning from heaven"* (Luke 10:18). When that happened, the earth experienced a cataclysm of the greatest magnitude, which destroyed all life on earth. According to the notes given to Genesis 1:2 in Dake's Annotated Reference Bible and the Scofield Bible, the text means that the earth was made waste and destroyed.[12] That is why a new creation was necessary, if life on earth was to be.

Satan now lives in exile in the sphere of the earth. That is why God never called the second day of recreating life on earth "good" (Genesis 1:6–8), while He did so for all the other days. This sphere where Satan is now housed is called the "firmament" (Genesis 1:6), a word which is also used to describe a jail. So Satan is held captive in the earth up to the air heaven surrounding the earth. That is why he can influence people to sin and rebel against God and His will.

Satan succeeded in taking along with him a third of the angels in his fall (Revelation 12:4). These are all acting as devils, evil spirits, and demons... and they are all around us. The impact they have on people begins with evil and negative thoughts and progresses to complete possession of their mind and willpower. The only protection and redemption we have against them is giving ourselves over to Jesus Christ and following Him closely. In Him, we are definitely safe against these evil forces. Those people who do not do this remain subjects of Satan and will share in his eternal fate after the great judgment day of God (Matthew 25:41 and Revelation 20:11–15).

---

[12] Dake, Finis Jennings. *Dake's Annotated Reference Bible*. Atlanta: Dake Bible Sales (1963), p. 1, note m. Also: Scofield, C.I. *The Scofield Reference Bible*. New York: Oxford University Press (1945), p. 3, note 3.

9.
GOD'S REDEMPTIVE WORK BEGINS

The first book of the Bible is Genesis, a Greek/Latin word meaning "beginning." There are many beginnings in Genesis: creation, sin, redemption, the genealogy of Christ's ancestors, etc. God's redemption effort begins with the creation of the Adamite race of mankind, at about 4000 B.C. The Negroid and Mongoloid races had gotten themselves somehow caught into the devil's tricks and needed redemption. The Apostle Paul refers to this: *"Nevertheless death reigned from Adam to Moses, <u>even over those who had not sinned according to the likeness of the transgression of Adam</u>"* (Romans 5:14, emphasis mine). Evidently the pre-Adamite people were subject to death long before Adam came along, as proven by archaeology. Adam was to be the beginning of redeeming people from sin and death, but he got himself in trouble as well by sinning against God's commandment, and came to require redemption himself.

Here is what happened next. God had created Adam out of red clay, which is why he was called Adam ("Red One"). In the Gospel of Luke, Adam is called "the son of God." He was placed in a garden that God had created for him, called Eden, situated somewhere between the Lebanon mountains in Syria and the foothills of the Iranian mountains, along the Euphrates and Tigris rivers of Iraq. Some scholars claim it was placed near the city of Eridu in the Euphrates valley. This garden contained all the fruit that is typically now found in Europe and Asia.

But Adam felt alone in the garden. According to Josephus, God let him see animals in their lovemaking, which made Adam want that, too. Therefore God put him to sleep and took a rib out of his body and made a woman out of it. Her name was Eve (meaning "Mother of all Living"). There is an interesting saying among Evangelicals: "God did not make Eve from Adam's foot, so he should step upon her, nor did he make her from Adam's head, so she should rule over him, but God made her from the heart area of Adam, so he should love, care and respect her, and not abuse her in any way."

Actually, the Germanic peoples treated their women like friends and comrades, not inferior to men, but equal in status. The idea that women are inferior to men came to northern Europe from the Mediterranean world, including from some sects of Israel, the Arabs, and the Roman Catholic Church. It was only in the twentieth century that women regained their original status.

Back to Adam and Eve. God had planted into the Garden of Eden two special trees: first, the Tree of the Knowledge of Good and Evil. The fruit of the Tree of Knowledge of Good and Evil would cause a person to recognize good and evil. God forbade Adam and Eve to eat of its fruit or to touch that tree. The other was the Tree of Life. It would revitalize people, so that they would not need to die. This

The Redemption Story

means that even Adam and Eve were not created imperishable, but mortal. Immortality was to be gained by obedience to God and eating of the Tree of Life. It was God's plan to use this tree for the benefit of all mankind.

This arrangement angered Satan, so he transformed himself into a serpent (spirits can do such things), and he talked kindly to Eve, causing her to distrust God. This was the beginning of sin of the Adamite race. She took its fruit, ate it, and gave some to her husband, and he too ate. This is what Paul called the "transgression of Adam": he loved his wife more than God (Romans 5:14). That is why he took the forbidden fruit out of her hand and ate it. As a result, Adam and Eve were exiled from the garden before they could ingest fruit from the Tree of Life, so eventually they would have to die. The Hebrew word for this means, "in dying they will die." So the dying process began with the act of sin.

In this story, God provides the first prophecy concerning the coming deliverer Jesus Christ. First, He punished the serpent by taking away his legs and feet, so he had to crawl as a snake. This was a personal punishment. (Bear in mind, that it does not follow that all snakes used to have legs, but lost them at that point in history.) Then Adam was told that the redeemer, called here "the Seed of the Woman," would crush the serpent's seed, the "Antichrist," at some point in the future. The remarkable thing is that the redeemer was not called a "Man's Seed," but a "Woman's Seed." This is a reference to the virgin birth of Jesus Christ, who had no earthly father, but was conceived by the Holy Spirit, while the "Serpent's Seed," also called "the Dragon" and "Antichrist," had no mother mentioned, but instead just a father: namely Satan, the Devil. It was first revealed to the early Church Fathers that a demon-possessed Jewish virgin would become the mother of Antichrist. He would copy Jesus Christ by also being born in Bethlehem, die a violent death, and go through a resurrection, so as to deceive many people and make them believe that he is the real Christ.

With the fall of Adam and Eve into sin, a long struggle began for peoples' souls between God and His angels and Satan and his angels. This struggle is still on going today and will last until the last person who is willing to accept Jesus Christ as his/her personal Saviour and Lord has done so. After that, the judgments of God will begin, and this old world will finally be shot away into the dark universe. A new earth will be created for all the saved people to live happily and eternally.

Some people ask, if there is a God of love, why does He tolerate all the injustices and horrendous things happening on the earth? The reason is that He has a plan for the ages that apparently cannot be altered until everything forecast by His prophets in the Bible has been fulfilled.

We can trust God to do the right things even if we cannot fully understand His ways. He said through the Prophet Isaiah, *"As the heavens are higher than the earth, so are My ways higher than your ways, and My thoughts than your thoughts"* (Isaiah 55:9). One thing we do know: since 80% of all biblical prophecies are said to have been fulfilled, and only 20% are still outstanding, we are far closer to the final day of judgment and deliverance than ever before—especially considering that many of these 80% have been fulfilled within the last two hundred years. The closer we get to the end, the faster it appears to come.

10.
THE HIGH POINTS OF THIS STRUGGLE BETWEEN GOD AND SATAN

Before I begin to trace the struggle between God and Satan concerning people, I would like to explain the details the Bible gives us regarding lifespans. It is unknown to me what the life expectancies were for the Negroid and Mongoloid peoples, because the Bible is silent on that topic. But for the Adamite people, this scheme appears: For the first 2500 years, the Adamite race began with a very long lifespan. Adam lived 930 years. The longest living person was Methuselah, who reached 969 years. Moses (who lived around 1500 B.C.) reached only 120 years. At about 600 B.C., the people in Israel were reaching an average age of fifty-six. At the time of Christ, women in Israel reached an average age of thirty-five. In about 1890, males in Sweden reached an average of thirty-five years as well, mainly because of an alcohol problem. In the rest of Europe, it came to about forty-eight. Since that time, life expectancy has been on the rise and will continue to do so. The Bible foresees a return to the long lives that the ancients used to enjoy once Jesus Christ returns to be the King and High Priest of the whole world. According to the Prophet Isaiah, a 100-year-old person will be called "a child" (Isaiah 65:20–23).

Now I will trace the struggle between good and evil for the souls of people. In Genesis 6, God became unhappy with the Adamite race. *"The Lord was sorry that He had made man [Adam and his descendants] on the earth. He was grieved in His heart"* (Genesis 6:6). Note that the "earth" in the Bible actually encompasses only the Mediterranean, Middle East and North African world. *"So the Lord said, 'I will destroy man... from the face of the earth'"* (Genesis 6:7).

This is what had happened: Some of the fallen angels acquired for themselves some organic material and assumed human physical qualities. They took themselves Adamite women, as many as they pleased for wives (polygamy). Their children became huge and mentally inferior persons whom the Bible refers to as the Nephilim ("giants, brutes"). Some of them reached twice the size of a normal person and had six fingers on each hand and six toes on each foot (2 Samuel 21). However, the average size of a normal person was five feet. This phenomenon, called gigantism, still exists occasionally today. For example, a woman by the name of Marianne Wehde (in Germany) was eight feet and four inches tall! Among the Palestinians are still a few families that show the abnormality of six fingers and six toes on each extremity. This trend of infiltrating the Adamite race with demonic influence advanced so far that only *one* family of the true and pure Adamites was left: the family of Noah

The Redemption Story

(Genesis 6:9). Thus Satan was hoping to destroy the divine decree of a coming Saviour, and he nearly made it! For the Redeemer was to come from Adam and Eve's seed, remember?

God's answer to this threat was a mighty flood, called the "Deluge." It happened around 2400 B.C. Its story can be found in Genesis 6–8. Evangelicals believe that this flood covered the whole earth as we know it today. As evidence, they claim the stories and myths of large-scale floods told by many nations on earth. However, they arrived at this conclusion through a misunderstanding of the term "earth," which really just refers to the Mediterranean region, or the known world at the time. Archaeology also confirms that neither the Negroids nor the Mongoloids suffered extinction, but instead show a continuous existence from many thousands of years ago through to the present day.

The flood God had in mind needed only to occur there, where the Nephilim lived, to extinguish that race of abnormal people. However, a very few of these people still escaped the Deluge. The last giants of this race were killed during the reign of King David (900 B.C.).

God instructed Noah to build a large ship called the Ark. It was to house Noah, his family, and pairs of local animal species that otherwise would be threatened with extinction. This ship was quite large. Its size was not matched until about 1850 A.D. It was built in the area of the Turkish city of Dogubiazit. There you can still see today the remains of the cribbage used during its construction. Archaeologists have found the wooden trusses of its wharf inside a ship-shaped formation of exactly the length the Bible provides us with. These wooden trusses were fastened with iron spikes predating the beginning of the Iron Age, in contrast of the view of some scientists. From that place, ten giant stone anchors have been found that are ten feet tall and are spread out in a line from Dogubiazit to Mount Ararat, twenty-five kilometres to the northeast. In 1955, a French industrialist by the name of Fernand Navarra and his son Raphael found the residue of the Ark in a shallow glacier lake near the summit of the larger Ararat peak. They cut a four-foot piece off and brought it home, where they let it be tested in both Spain and Egypt. The wood type was of a species of oak and age that matched the requirements for the building of Noah's Ark. So here you have a series of evidences that an early Bible story is archaeologically proven. It just goes to show that you can trust the Bible!

11.
A New Beginning

The story of the great flood is told from Noah's view and experience. He did not see any other mountains sticking out of the waters, which is why he figured that the whole earth was drowned. A man can see about thirty-five kilometres around himself on flat terrain. One can see high mountains from about 120 kilometres away. In theology, we call what people see, experience, and talk about in the

Bible as the Subjective View. Things that God says directly or through the prophets we call the Objective View. Most Christians never take these facts in consideration when they assess the extent of the Deluge. Also, the Middle East has seen some significant transformation throughout the thousands of years that have passed since Noah's time.

The flood lasted close to one year. However, Noah stayed in the Ark until the twenty-seventh day of the second month. When Noah made animal sacrifices for God, Yahweh made the Noahic Covenant with him:

1. No more destruction of the earth through a flood.
2. People can eat anything they find to eat.

Before this time, there were different dietary rules. The Negroids and Mongoloids could eat fruits and herbs. The Adamites, as long as they lived in the Garden of Eden, were told to eat fruits. After the fall of the Adamites into sin, herbs were added to their diet. Now everything edible was permitted to be eaten, especially meats. The reason for this is simple, for there was practically nothing on earth to be eaten right after the flood. Indeed, there was little choice of food except for water creatures apart from the leftovers of the ark.

3. As a reminder of that covenant, God appointed the rainbow.

How did the flood come about in the first place? God let it rain on earth and opened *"the fountains of the great deep"* (Genesis 7:11–12).

Many Christians believe that it did not rain before this great flood anywhere on the earth as we know the earth today. This, however, is a mistake. It is true that God did not let it rain in the area called Eden—otherwise Adam and Eve would have been soaked by rain from time to time. They lived in the garden, but had no other shelter. They needed none, because of the climate existing there. But God had the Garden of Eden watered by a river (Genesis 2:10), and rivers come about through precipitation, especially in mountainous areas, and often through glaciers. So there had to have been rain or snow in the parts of the world that the ancient Adamites did not know anything about. They had no conception of the true size of the earth.

Noah's family consisted of his wife, three sons, and their wives. Their descendants first repopulated "the earth" (Mediterranean world, North Africa, and the Middle East). Japhet, the youngest son, was the father of the Caucasians. These people migrated as far east as India, and to the north they covered Europe. One Caucasian tribe, the Ainus, travelled across Asia to the north of Japan, and from there they went over to Alaska and mixed themselves with the Mongoloid aboriginals of North America. This is why many Indians in the northern half of North America have Caucasian DNA mixed with their own.

Noah's oldest son, Shem, whose great-grandson was Eber, was the father of the Hebrews and the Arabs living in the Middle East.

The middle son, Ham, was the father of the Ethiopians of North Africa. Six hundred years later, the Caucasians already occupied my homeland, the state of Hesse in Germany. For example, near to where my family lived is a large stone box grave, found in 1905 in a field by a plough that hit one of its stones in the soil. It has an entrance hole at one end drilled through a stone slab. According to scientific findings, twenty-eight families were buried there, and there were wheat and apple seeds in the communal grave. This grave originates from 2000 B.C., the time of biblical Abraham.

The story of Noah and the Great Deluge is also testified to by a number of well-known ancient writers. Among them are Berosus the Chaldean, Hieronymus the Egyptian, Mnaseas, Nicolaus of Damascus, and many more.

12.
THE GREAT CONFUSION

Genesis 11 is intimately connected with Chapters 10 and 12. Before commenting on Chapter 10, though, one must first describe some of the happenings in Chapter 11: the story of how the Noahic family and their descendants moved away from the landing place of the Ark on Mount Ararat in the Armenian part of Turkey, above the Agora valley. In his descent from the mountain, Noah settled down 115 kilometres southeast from Ararat in a place called

Nachicevan, which still exists as a small city today. Its name means "the first place of descent," and it claims to have Noah's tomb.

According to Josephus, a Jewish writer of the time of Christ who reflects Jewish historical tradition, God ordered the descendants of Noah to spread out in many directions, but they did not obey. Instead, they moved back all together to the Eden area between the Tigris and Euphrates rivers in Iraq. One of their descendants, a man by the name of Nimrod, became the first king to reign over a number of cities and their lands. He was a tyrant. Other kings of antiquity ruled merely over one city and its lands, but Nimrod desired to command much more.

Nimrod rebelled against God and wanted to build a tower that would withstand another deluge and save his people. This place was called Babel, and later Babylon, the capital city of the Chaldeans. The country was also called the Babylonian Empire, and it ruled the territory of modern day Iraq. The name Babel means "Confusion," because God confused the different races present there by changing their speech suddenly, so that they could not understand each other and had to give up the construction of the tower.

These people had used burned bricks to build the tower, which was quite an accomplishment considering that even today in many places in the Middle East and Africa people still build dwellings from sundried bricks. Babylon's ruins are located ninety kilometres south of Baghdad, the capital of Iraq. During his time, Saddam Hussein began to rebuild the city.

The Redemption Story 35

It appears that the descendants of Noah could write and had gathered an astounding amount of knowledge in geometry and astronomy. In fact, it appears that the pre-flood fathers already discovered the Great Astronomical Year, consisting of six hundred solar years. They could only have discovered this through living such fantastically long lives. They also must have had strong technological information to attempt such a giant building project as the Ark of Noah.

Chapter 10 describes the distribution of Adamite races after God destroyed the Tower of Babel. Of interest to me is the descendancy of Japhet, the youngest son of Noah, whose line flows down through time to the *Ashkenazim*, the Hebrew word for Germans. Also interesting is the fact that no Negroid or Mongoloid races are mentioned in the list of Noah's descendants, which confirms my presentation of the creation of these races in Genesis 1 as the oldest human races. It also confirms the fact that they were not touched by the Deluge. The Adamites came in contact with these peoples later in history.

Important for the further development of the Bible and the coming of our Saviour is the beginning of the Hebrew race through Noah's first son, Shem. He became the father of the Semites: the Arabs and Jews. The Jews in turn come from Shem's great-grandson Eber, or "Heber," resulting in the name Hebrews. Today, when living in Palestine, we call them "Israelis." From this point onward, God gave up on speaking to the existing human races and focused on the Hebrews. He began to build a separate nation, which He claimed as His very own through one special Hebrew man named Abram, beginning from Genesis 12.

13.

ABRAHAM, THE MAN OF FAITH

Abram (his given name) was born about 292 years after the Deluge, around 2165 B.C. The extensive information we have of him comes primarily from Genesis 12–25, though we also have some ancient accounts through writers like Josephus.

Abraham's father, Terah, was a manufacturer of clay idols that people bought to protect their homes from evil. This is something people still do in many countries, even in Canada of today. These idols continued to bear Terah's name, and eventually came to be called "Teraphim." Somehow, Abram must have come in contact with people who worshipped Yahweh, also called the *"God Most High, Possessor of heaven and earth"* (Genesis 14:19). These were people who kept the traditions of belief in Yahweh after the Great Flood.

Abram was a very intelligent man and understood that manmade idols were a great nonsense. One day, he became very angry with his father and his idols so that he smashed them in a rage and said that there was just one God in the universe and no one else, the God who had brought their ancestors through the Flood. God responded to Abram, not just because of his demonstration of belief, but also because Abram had a soft heart and a good character. The Bible says that Yahweh spoke and physically appeared to him several times. Abram learned to put his trust in Him. Yahweh accounted this act of faith to Abram as being right in line with God's thinking and expectation. This is what Christians call "righteousness" today.

Abram's hometown was the city of Ur, an important shipping centre of the ancient world situated at the end of the Persian Gulf. It had two harbours, as well as a great temple of the moon idols Nannar and Ningal. It had a school for children. Its houses were very comfortable in a very pleasant climate. The city even had a sewage system.

One day, for some reason, Terah moved with his family to Haran. Imagine the sacrifice Terah and his family made by traveling northward along the Euphrates valley and up to a hot and primitive semi-desert town called Haran, in today's Syria! In Haran, Terah died. Then God called Abram with these words: *"Get out of your country, from your relatives and from your father's house, to a land that I will show you. I will make you to a great nation; I will bless you and make your name great; and you shall be a blessing. I will bless those who bless you, and I will curse him who curses you; and in you all the families of the earth shall be blessed"* (Genesis 12:1–3). Abram obeyed.

Abram was seventy-five years old when he was called by God and emigrated to follow His leading.

Abram continued his migration to Palestine, called Canaan at that time. This land is known as the Holy Land because God wanted to use it to bring about the Redeemer of mankind, Jesus Christ. There, God appeared to Abram again and told him that this was the land his descendants were going to inherit.

Abram became rich with sheep and other domesticated animals, living in Canaan as a nomad moving with his livestock as needed. The Letter to the Hebrews writes that Abram himself did not regard Canaan his final home, but instead *"waited for the city which has foundations, whose builder and maker is God"* (Hebrews 11:10).

In Canaan, he eventually met a priest of the God Most High named Melchizedek. About this man there is no known information of family, birth or death, and because of this he is held to be a "type" who foreshadows Jesus Christ, who as God's Son has no beginning or end of life (Hebrews 7:3).

In Canaan, God made with Abram a covenant, a treaty, that contained a promise: He promised him a son through whom his descendants would become a special nation, owning this land of Canaan. He foretold Abram that his descendants would first have to suffer as slaves in a different nation for four hundred years. At that time, the measure of sins of the Canaanites would be fulfilled and Abram's descendants would conquer Canaan and annihilate the Canaanites. This sounds very cruel, but God had a reason for doing such a terrible thing—the sins of the Canaanites were such that God could not allow them to continue to exist, else they would affect the rest of mankind with their sins and sicknesses. Some of the sins mentioned were:

> 1. They worshipped idols and offered their sons and daughters as human blood sacrifices in

The Redemption Story

       their temples. After killing their children, they would burn them to ashes.
2. They killed some of their babies, placed the little bodies into clay vessels, and built them into the walls of their homes. These people believed that their dead babies in the walls of their houses would act as protecting spirits for their homes and families.
3. They employed temple prostitutes, both female and male, thereby spreading immorality and diseases.
4. They practised homosexuality, which is an abomination to God.
5. There still existed a few Nephilim that somehow had escaped the Great Deluge and needed to be destroyed. These had moved into the Holy Land from the mountainous East.

With the descendants of the Nephilim, Satan populated the borderlands of Canaan with giants to prevent God's people from entering into it. It would take a miracle for the Israelites to take this country for themselves. All this left God no choice but to become radical. We learn from this story that God takes sin very seriously. We in our age will not escape His punishment once the measure of sin is fulfilled in our world today. Therefore it is necessary for whoever listens and understands, and wants to escape the judgment of God, to repent from their personal sins and accept Jesus Christ as their personal Saviour and Lord.

Abram believed God, which pleased Him. He accounted Abram's trust as righteousness. Therefore He changed Abram's name to Abraham, meaning "Father of a great multitude." At that time, Abraham was ninety-nine years old and still had no son. His wife was ten years younger and way beyond her child bearing years, but Abraham still trusted God to keep His promise. As a sign of this covenant, God commanded Abraham and all males under his authority to be circumcised. That meant to cut the foreskin off their penises, which was to demonstrate that Abraham and his descendants were different people in nature than all other people living on the earth. The Jews still do this today.

At ninety years of age, Sarai, whose name was changed to "Sarah," meaning "princess," gave birth to their son Isaac. Without question, this was a miracle birth, and so the origin of the Jewish people came about through a miracle. The name Isaac means "laughter." He got that name, I suppose, because it was really funny that an old man of a hundred years and an old woman of ninety years should have a child.

Abraham had a son before Isaac, however, but Sarah was not the mother. Instead, he had lain with one of his slave girls, named Hagar. Sarah set him up to do this, but later rejected both mother and son, whose name was Ishmael. This was hard for Abraham, but God told him to let it happen, so he sent mother and son away. Ishmael was not the son whom God had in mind to be the heir of God's promises and covenant with Abraham. Isaac was. He was the promised "Seed."

Previous to this, God had once commanded Abraham to look into the starry sky where the constellation Virgo ("Virgin") was dominant. In one hand, the image of the virgin carries a seed, and in the other a branch. This is a stellar event that happens every August. God told him that so would Abraham's future seed be: a child born of a virgin. This was fulfilled in the virgin birth of Jesus Christ.

God honoured Abraham with His compassion by forgiving the mistake he had made with the slave girl and promised to bless Ishmael, too, for Abraham's sake. Ishmael became the first father of the Arabs. There has been friction between the Ishmaelites and Israelites ever since, as can be evidenced any day by turning on the news and listening to unfolding events concerning the state of Israel and its Arab neighbours. It all came about because of Abraham's mistake with Hagar. This conflict will continue until the return of Jesus Christ, who will bring us peace for the whole world. After Sarah's death, Abraham married a woman named Keturah. He had six sons with her, who all became part of the Arab world. Abraham died when he reached 175 years.

Abraham, the "Friend of God," has a far-reaching influence not only because of his natural descendants, the Israelis and the Arabs and their conflict, but also because of the covenant and promise of God to let him be a blessing to all nations. This He accomplished through the coming of Jesus Christ into this world, and the blessing will continue through Jesus.

Abraham's faith and trust in Almighty God became a pattern for us all. God accepts people who show the same type of faith in Him as Abraham did, treating them as His own spiritual sons and daughters. Any person, regardless of race, gender, nationality, or load of sins who puts his/her trust in Jesus Christ, God's only begotten Son, is regarded by God as a member of His divine family. That person will be endued with eternal life in the eternal presence of God. The Apostle Paul calls Jesus therefore *"the firstborn among many brethren"* (Romans 8:29).

Just think, the eternal Son of God, who came down to this rotten world and received the name Jesus, which means "Saviour"—in regards to His earthly existence and ministry—will be your Great Brother. He gave His life for you so that your sins might be forgiven for all eternity, so that you may live forever with Him in all happiness! That is awesome! Surely He deserves our unending love and faithfulness.

14.

God's Plan of Redemption Continued

One of the twin sons that Isaac and his wife Rebekah had was named Jacob. His history covers Genesis 25–50. His name means "Heel catcher," often explained as "Deceiver," because of some of the things he did in his life. But God eventually got through to him, because of the promise and covenant God had made with his grandfather Abraham. Jacob ended up having four wives, with whom he had a total of twelve sons, who became the tribe fathers of the nation of Israel.

Jacob had a number of encounters with God. The one encounter that really changed his life was when God came down physically one night and wrestled with Jacob. It happened when Jacob's life was at its lowest point (Genesis 32:22–32). That night, God changed Jacob's name and character from "Deceiver" to "Israel," meaning variously "God fighter" and "Prince with God." Of the twelve sons Jacob had, two are outstanding persons: Judah and Joseph. To Judah it was prophesied that through his tribe the Messiah, meaning "the Anointed," would come. This term pointed toward Jesus Christ, the deliverer, who would eventually come.

15.

JOSEPH, GOD'S MAN OF ACTION

Jacob's other important son was Joseph. He was a spiritual person from youth onward. God gave him visions that concerned the future of Jacob's family.

Because Jacob loved Joseph more than all his other sons, his brothers hated him. They sold him to Arab merchants, who in turn sold him to the captain of the royal guards of the king of Egypt, called the "Pharaoh." The captain's name was Potiphar. God blessed Joseph in his service to his master, and so Joseph became the head slave, the steward of Potiphar's estate. Joseph was a very wise and handsome looking young man, which caused Potiphar's wife to fall in love with him. She once grabbed him for sex, but Joseph left his outer coat with her and ran away from her. She took her revenge on him and accused him of rape, which landed Joseph in prison. But once again, Joseph proved the quality of his character while in jail, so much so that he gained the confidence of the jail keeper, who left him to handle all the prison's business.

In jail, Joseph met Pharaoh's baker and cupbearer, who had troubling dreams that Joseph interpreted for them. As predicted by Joseph, the cupbearer was reinstated by Pharaoh to serve him.

Some time later, Pharaoh found himself plagued with a couple of troubling dreams. The cupbearer, remembering Joseph, told Pharaoh about the dream interpreter he had encountered in prison. The king had Joseph come to the palace, where he told Joseph about his dreams, and Joseph interpreted them correctly.

16.

PHARAOH'S DREAMS

You will find these dreams in Genesis 41. Pharaoh dreamed that he was standing by the River Nile. Out of the water came seven fat cows, and after them came seven gaunt ones. These last seven cows ate up the fat cows. Pharaoh's second dream was this: seven healthy ears of grain grew on a single stalk. After them came seven thin ears of grain scorched by the east wind and they swallowed up the seven healthy ones. None of Pharaoh's wise men and magicians could interpret these dreams. Through the cupbearer's words, Joseph was called on to interpret these dreams.

Joseph said that both dreams dealt with the same issue: seven good harvest years would be followed by seven years of draught. Joseph recommended that Pharaoh procure himself a wise man to oversee the collection of the surplus of the seven good harvests. That way, the people would have something to eat during the following seven meagre years and not perish.

Pharaoh felt that since Joseph was wise enough to interpret these dreams, he would also be the wisest man to take care of the surplus harvest program. He promoted Joseph to be the second in command of Egypt. Joseph successfully accomplished this task.

> **Egyptian wheat**
>
> Egyptian hieroglyphs show grain stalks with seven ears. This is more than modern wheat produces, which goes to show that people were very intelligent at that time, and in some areas perhaps even more advanced than us moderns! In my day, I have seen four-eared wheat stalks in Saskatchewan.

When the dry years came, Jacob and his family felt the effect of the famine which had also hit their area in Palestine. Hearing that there was grain in Egypt, Jacob sent his sons to there to buy grain for their families. When his brothers appeared before him, Joseph recognized them... though they did not recognize Joseph. He dealt harshly with them, not for the sake of revenge, but to test their characters. This happened a couple of times more. Finally, he made himself known to them, which caused a scene of repentance, forgiveness, and reconciliation. He then had his family move to Egypt at the invitation of Pharaoh. Jacob was 130 years old when he and his family moved to Egypt proper.

I say "Egypt proper," because the land Abraham and his descendants Isaac and Jacob already were living in was actually considered Egyptian territory, just like the Northwest Territories are to Canada. They had lived there for 215 years, in the area of Beer Shebah. This territory covers the whole Sinai peninsula, up to a part of the future state of Judah. Jacob's family remained in Egypt proper another 430 years, for four generations (Genesis 15:16, Exodus 12:40–41). This gives us thirty years more than the four hundred years God had revealed to Abraham in Genesis 15:13. It appears that God counted these years from when Abraham's

The Redemption Story

family exited from the city of Haran, where they had lived a number of years. God called Abraham to leave this city when he was seventy-five years old. From Abraham to Moses, there were a total of seven generations living under Egyptian authority.

Some Israelites were always keeping an exact record of their generations, even beyond the time of Christ, and a few Jewish families may still be in possession of their original genealogy today. This conclusion can be arrived at when one reads the books of Esra, Nehemiah, and the prophet Zechariah (Chapters 10 and 11). Zechariah refers primarily to the family of King David. It was last mentioned in history in 1539 A.D. Some Jewish circles know where they are. From this family Jesus came, and from this family will come the last governor of modern day Israel before Christ's return.

Another family that is still in existence today is the priestly family of Zadok. Its ancestry is not held secret. Members of that family live in the United States, Canada, and Israel, and they are actively involved with the rebuilding plans for the new temple. Only a member of that family will be allowed to be High Priest of the future temple services.

A short time after the Israelites moved into the province Goshen of

> **Jewish midwives**
>
> Of interest is the way the Israelite women gave birth to their children. They sat on a "birth stool," not lying in bed like modern women do. Doctors today agree that the birth stool method of giving birth is a lot easier on women, since the weight of the baby pulls itself downward.

Egypt proper, the governing family of Egypt was dethroned and another family came into power, also under the title of Pharaoh. However, this family forgot the blessings that the Israelite Joseph had been to Egypt, and they began to enslave the Israelites and make them serve with rigor.

They wanted to keep the Israelites from multiplying and so ordered all newborn Jewish baby boys killed. The Jewish midwives refused to comply with that order.

17.

The Man God Used to Bring Liberty to Israel

One of the little boys saved was Moses, the son of Amram and his wife Jochebed of the tribe of Levi. When he was three months old, his mother could not hide him anymore. She constructed a box of bulrushes and pitch and let her daughter Miriam lay it among the reeds of the River Nile and observe what would happen to him. He was discovered by Pharaoh's daughter, who was bathing nearby. This woman had compassion on the baby and took him to be her son. She called him "Moses," meaning "drawn from the water." She raised Moses at Pharaoh's palace, and Moses was accepted by all as an Egyptian prince. He was appointed a general in Egypt's war with Ethiopia.

18.

MOSES' SPIRITUAL AWAKENING

According to Josephus, Moses had a very good and gentle character. The Bible says that he was a very meek person. In the war against Ethiopia, which he won, the Princess Tharbis of Ethiopia was so enthused about Moses' character that she fell in love with him and he married her. She was his first wife. In the book of Numbers (the fourth book of Moses), the Israelites were murmuring against Moses for having this Ethiopian wife (Numbers 12:1).

When Moses was forty years old, somehow he became aware that he was a Hebrew himself by birth and he took a keen interest in the suffering of the Israelites in Egypt, who were building some cities. When he saw an Egyptian slave driver beating a Hebrew, Moses got so angry that he killed the slave driver. This became known to the Pharaoh, forcing Moses to flee out of Egypt.

The fastest way out of Egypt was the "Arabian way," which led past Ezion-Geber at the end of the Gulf of Aquaba into Midian. In Midian, he became a shepherd for the Priest Jethro Reuel. He married one of his daughters, named Zipporah, who became his second wife. With her he had a son named Gershom.

One day, as he kept watch over his sheep, he noticed a strange sight up on the mountain called Sinai. A bush was burning, but was not consumed by the fire. Becoming curious, he went up on the mountain into the close presence of that burning bush.

Suddenly he heard a voice speaking to him out of the fire of the bush: "Moses, Moses..." He immediately understood that this was Yahweh talking to him. Yahweh told him to return to Egypt and to lead the Israelites out of Egypt into the Promised Land, Canaan. Moses refused at first and it took quite a challenge from God for Moses to accept this call. God promised him to be with him with great miracles and signs, for no man on his own would be able to accomplish such a feat. Moses was eighty years old at the time.

Finally, he accepted God's call and went with his wife and sons back to Egypt. The authorities who would have had him executed for killing the Egyptian had all died in the meantime. God ordered Moses' brother Aaron to meet him in the desert. At his arrival in Goshen in Egypt, where the Israelites were kept as slaves, Moses met with their elders and they trusted him.

19.
THE DELIVERER AT WORK

Moses and Aaron went to see the Pharaoh. They spoke to him in the name of the God of the Hebrews. They challenged Pharaoh to let Israel go, to have a feast and sacrifice in the desert, but Pharaoh resisted.

God was with Moses and allowed him to perform many miracles. Pharaoh's priests copied some of them, until they finally had to give up. At the point of the third plague, they told Pharaoh, *"This is the finger of God"* (Exodus 8:19).

But Pharaoh did not listen.

God punished the Egyptians with a number of miracle plagues to move Pharaoh to yield, but he remained stubborn. These are the plagues God sent upon them:

1. Changing the waters of Egypt into blood.
2. Flooding the land with frogs.
3. Flooding the land with lice.
4. Flooding the land with flies.
5. Killing Egypt's livestock with a very severe pestilence.
6. Causing a breakout of boils on man and beast.

7. Flooding the land with hail.
8. Flooding the land with locusts.
9. Covering Egypt with a supernatural darkness.

The part of Egypt where the Hebrews lived was spared from these plagues. Pharaoh remained stubborn. But then followed the final plague, which finally made Pharaoh let Israel go.

10. The killing of the firstborn of all animals and people. Even Pharaoh's own son died that night.

Israel was ordered by God that each family should kill a lamb and take some of its blood and paint it on the sides and the lintel of the doorframes of their homes. This would be the sign for the Angel of Death to pass over them and not harm them. The Israelites were ordered to eat unleavened bread and dress into travel clothes.

Pharaoh gave the order to let Israel go out of the country. God ordered that henceforth Israel should celebrate this day of their freedom with lamb's meat and unleavened bread every year on the same day. That is why the Jews today continue to celebrate the Passover feast annually. The day Israel moved out of Egypt was 430 years, to the exact day. Apparently Israel kept very good records to show this.

Once Israel was on the move, they asked their Egyptian neighbours for items of value and jewellery, which they gladly gave them. A mixed multitude of non-Hebrew slaves also seized the opportunity and fled with the Hebrews to freedom.

Israel also owned a lot of livestock. This is a very important factor to consider when seeking to determine which route they took out of Egypt, for their livestock and the mass of people, estimated to be up to three million, needed a great deal of food and water. God had ordered Moses to bring Israel to Mount Sinai, where He had appeared to Moses in the burning bush in the first place, to receive further instructions.

First Israel went south to where the city Ismailia is now, but they were ordered by God to turn north to where the ruins of Etham or Kawm Gafanah Daphne are currently situated. This causes a problem for those who would have Israel cross the Red Sea near Suez through the Gulf of Suez. This route is simply not possible, given God's orders to turn north.

It also does not seem possible that the crossing could have taken place across the Gulf of Aqaba, on the other side of the Sinai Peninsula, as has been suggested by some. First, the Israelites would have had to cross through the borders of Egypt proper along the present Suez route, which was heavily fortified by the Egyptian military, and there is no hint of such a conflict at this point in Israel's flight. Second, the distance from the proposed Aqaba crossing to Mount Sinai is too short to match the sixty-day journey suggested by the Biblical account. Third, the Gulf of Aqaba is too wide—it would have taken longer than one night for three million people to cross. The fourth reason is that the Gulf is far too deep to facilitate a crossing. The descent would be incredibly steep, dipping up to at least two hundred meters below sea level.

Rather, they ended up at the shore of what today is called the Reed Sea, to a place named Etham. The area has suffered some change over the millennia by desert winds that poured sand into it. This is explained further in the next chapter.

This all leads to much discussion on where exactly the Israelites crossed over to the Sinai Peninsula. In addition, the Egyptians had already at that time a canal from Suez in the south to the Buhayrat Manzilah Lagoon in the north, which was used as a frontier wall against desert raiders, as well as for shipping. So crossing this canal would also have been a very difficult feat to manage.

There are a lot of considerations to take into account before one can be somewhat confident in describing the route of Israel's exit out of Egypt. I will try to discuss these points here:

1. The traditional route pointing southward into the peninsula to its southern tip must be contested because of the following observations:
   a) The route is very difficult because of great distances between the "wadis" (temporary watersheds that look like rivers only during and shortly after the rainy season, but otherwise are dry).
   b) The western lands of Sinai contain ancient copper and jewel stone mines.

They were operated by the Egyptians using slaves and the area was well-secured by the Egyptian military. It would not have been a good choice for the Israelites to go that way.

c) The exodus took place in the spring, in the period of March, April, and May, a time when rain showers still come and shallow water wells can be dug in the wadis.

2. Moses had already fled Egypt once before, travelling the fast route to Midian. He would now choose the same route. I have checked the Sinai Peninsula for wadis and opportunities to feed livestock during the crossing of the Sinai Wilderness. I found that the best and fastest route of escape from Egypt follows what the Bible calls "the Way of the Red Sea," in the direction of the Gulf of Aqaba at the east side of the peninsula, also called the "Arabian Highway."

In my opinion, they went from the area of Lake Timsah, which may be the Lake Marah of Exodus 15:23, and followed that road leading to Ezion-Geber at the end of the gulf. Twice did Israel gripe due to lack of water. There are only two areas along this route where one cannot travel to find water within one day. One of them is the area around Lake Timsah, which is a salt lake, and the other is in the desert of Paran. The third water conflict occurred at another time and place.

Now, where did Israel cross from Egypt proper into the Sinai Wilderness? I mentioned Etham and the Reed Sea. But the Bible says they crossed the Red Sea, so how do we solve this problem? Easily. The waters from the Red Sea penetrated the Egyptian canal right up to the Mediterranean Sea. This is so because the current of the high tide waters is higher in the Gulf of Suez than in the Mediterranean Sea. The speed of that current is half a mile per hour. So at Etham, Israel crossed Red Sea waters to get into the Sinai Peninsula.

20.
How Did Israel Do It?

While the Israelites, according to the Bible, camped at Etham in the northeastern part of Egypt proper, at the shores of the Reed Sea, Pharaoh had a change of mind and decided to return the Israelites back into slavery. He went after them with his army. When at evening the people saw the Egyptian army approaching, they blamed Moses for their upcoming misfortune and began to panic. Moses, however, looked up to the Lord God, who told him to stretch his staff over the sea. At that point, God sent a very strong wind to part the waters of the Reed Sea.

The Redemption Story

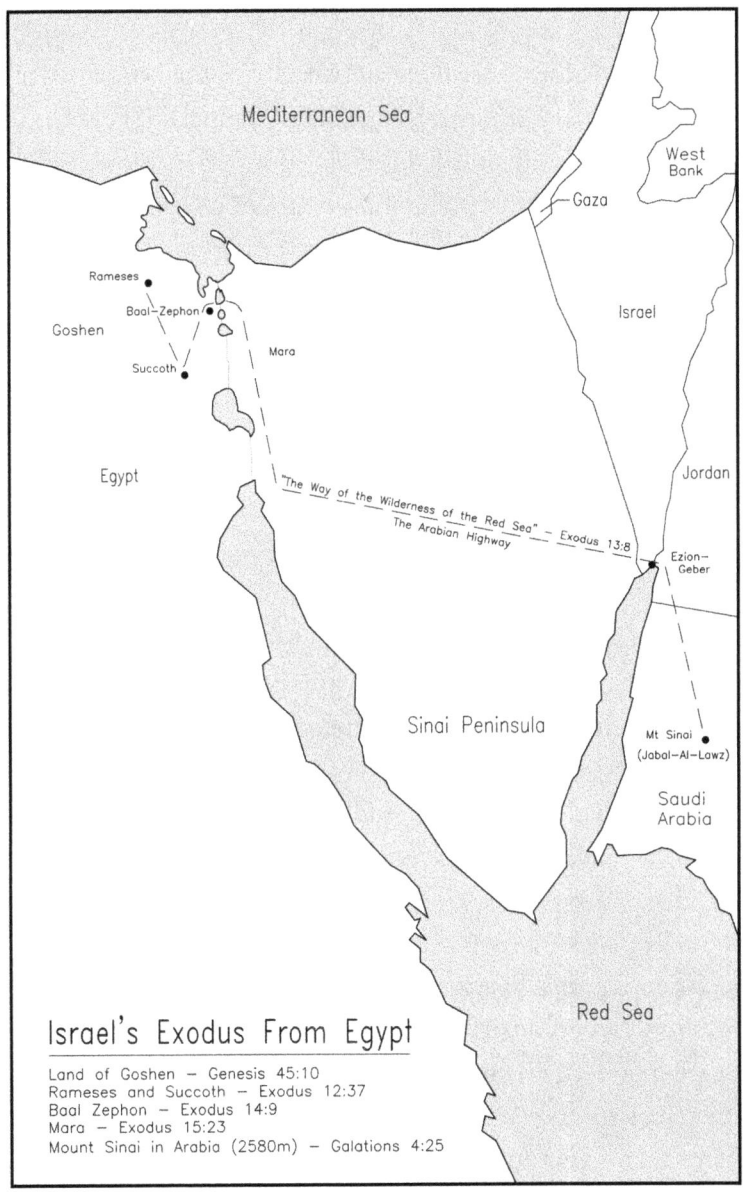

Moses led the Israelites through this cleared sea bottom over to the other side. This apparently took all night to accomplish. Pharaoh's army went in after them. Then God's presence appeared in a large cloud positioned between the fleeing people and the Egyptian army. Towards the Israelites' side, the cloud was lit up very brightly, so the people saw where they placed their feet. Toward the Egyptian army, it spread utter darkness, and this slowed them down, so that both groups never came in contact with each other during the whole night. When the last Hebrew reached the far shore, God turned the wind around and the sea waves from the north and south smashed against each other and swallowed up the Egyptian army. No Egyptian escaped.

This story poses some questions that need to be answered. First, the sea. It was actually, as I mentioned before, a large lagoon. Since there were reeds growing in it, it could not have been much deeper than about six feet. Further, the dry path along the sea bottom must have been very wide, so that the wind would not touch the fleeing Hebrews. The distance between one shore and the other must also have been narrow to allow three million people plus their livestock to make the crossing within twelve hours. Considering the livestock, as well as old people and children, the speed of the fleeing Israelites could not have been much faster than three kilometres per hour. The distance they had to travel has been estimated by some to be no more than five kilometres.

The mood among the Israelites after the crossing was done was one of jubilation, but this didn't last. Before long, the complaints started against Moses and God for water and

The Redemption Story

food. The stretch from the sea crossing to the first wadi took more than one day, so it's no surprise that everybody grew hungry and thirsty. Moses cleared the bitter waters of Marah by a miracle and God sent them "bread from heaven," in the form of a substance called manna. It was a small round substance looking like frost on the ground (Exodus 16:14). The people were called upon to gather enough of it for a single day. In Psalm 78:25, the psalm writer calls it "Angels' food." God even sent them meat in the form of birds called quails. In the Sinai Wilderness, only two plant varieties grow that are edible, so there wasn't much to help supplement the people's diets.

The story of Israel's escape from Egypt has had a strong impact on the Jewish people to this day. It is often referred to in the rest of the Bible, and it is commemorated annually in the Jewish Passover Feast.

Are there any proofs that this story actually happened? Of the crossing itself there is no physical evidence to be found. Desert sands often blow into this area from the western desert, and they have now blown for more than three thousand years. They have covered the remains of the evidences, such as pieces of Egyptian chariots and horse or human bone remains. However, there are evidences in the Sinai Wilderness of Israel's travels, such as writings on rock surfaces. They tell of some of the fortunes of the Israelites in the "Lust Graves" at Kibroth Hattaavah. There, the wrath of God killed many Israelites because of their constant murmurings against God. Moses had a tough job leading Israel to Mount Sinai to receive God's instructions.

Now, where is the real Mount Sinai located? According to the story, Israel never went to the southern tip of the Sinai Peninsula, where the traditional Mount Sinai is located. The Bible gives us a clear answer for this. It is just about unbelievable that so many Christians of the past have made the mistake of placing Mount Sinai at the southern tip of the peninsula. The Apostle Paul says very clearly in his letter to the Galatians, for everyone to understand that "Mount Sinai [is] in Arabia" (Galatians 4:25).

In the twentieth century, several groups of archaeologists found this mountain in Arabia. The area where it is located was called Midian in ancient days, according to the Bible. There Moses had found a new home and lived the life of a shepherd. The mountain is called Jabal al Lawz by the Arabs. It is 2580 feet tall. The Arabs have always known that this is the real Mount Sinai. They have built a high fence around its territory and assigned armed guards keep an eye on it.

Recently, men of the Wyatt Archaeological Research Center have succeeded in sneaking into this closed compound. They found clear evidences there to claim that this is indeed the true Mount Sinai. The twelve boundary stones of Exodus 19:12 are still there. So is the altar for the offering of animals. So is a creek bed. So is the blackness of the mountaintop, which is not caused by any volcanic eruption. The mountain is not a volcano. The black colouring of the rock was caused by the fiery presence of Yahweh on that mountain, as told in Exodus 19:16–20. Also visible there is the cave in which the prophet Elijah hid on his flight from Queen Jezebel of Israel.

At its foot there is a wide plain large enough to accommodate three million people. Such space is seriously lacking at the false Mount Sinai in the south of the Sinai Peninsula. So there is little doubt now where the true Mount Sinai is located.

21.
THE IMPORTANT EVENTS THAT IMPACT US LIVING TODAY

After exactly sixty days from the exit out of Egypt proper, Israel finally arrived at Mount Sinai in Arabia. Their average speed was six kilometres a day. This is reasonable due to the daily grazing time needed by the animals. They arrived at Mount Sinai just as the hot season began, about the beginning of June (Exodus 19).

In order to encounter the very presence of God, they had to wash their clothes in the waters of the nearby wadi. They also had to refrain from sexual intercourse two days ahead. Moses was ordered to set the boundary stones, which no person nor animal was allowed to pass. On the third day, there was thundering and lightning and a thick cloud on the mountaintop. A very loud trumpet then sounded. This experience caused the people to shake in fear. Moses led the people out from their camp to the foot of the mountain. After that, Yahweh came down upon it in fire. The whole mountain shook.

Moses spoke to God, and Yahweh answered him by voice. Then God gave them his covenant with Israel consisting of:
1. The ten basic commandments,
2. The civil laws, and
3. The ceremonial laws and ordinances.

The Ten Commandments were, in short:

1. You shall have no other gods.
2. You shall not make yourself any carved image or any likeness to resemble a god. (The people were not to make themselves any figure or painted representation to be worshipped as a god, whether that image was intended to represent an idol in heaven, on earth, or under the waters of the earth.)
3. You shall not take the name of Yahweh your God in vain (especially as a curse word).
4. You shall keep the Sabbath day holy. (That is our Saturday. No one was to work on that day. All were to rest and use that day for worshipping Yahweh.)
5. You shall honour father and mother, so you would live long on the earth.
6. You shall not murder.
7. You shall not commit any immorality.

The Redemption Story

8. You shall not steal.
9. You shall not lie against your neighbour.
10. You shall not covet (desire to take for yourself) anything that belongs to your neighbour, be it persons, animals or things.

The Israelites were terrified by hearing God's voice. They asked Moses not to let God speak to them, lest they would die for fear. God asked Moses to come up to the mountaintop. There he would receive the ten commandments, written by God's own hand on stone tablets. The rewards for keeping God's laws were long lives, many blessings, and protection from any evil by God Himself.

He also gave Moses a lot of good civil and religious laws for Israel. Among them are:

1. Regulations regarding slavery: Humane treatment of slaves and limitations of slavery.
2. Regulations regarding crime control and justice.
3. Regulations regarding the treatment of animals.
4. Regulations regarding morality:
   a) No sex before marriage.
   b) No homosexuality.
   c) No sex during a woman's period of menstruation. It was considered unclean.

While the menstruation itself only lasts about five days, a woman is normally fertile beginning on the twelfth day from the start of her menstruation. God wanted Israel to have many children in order for the nation to grow, and sex before that day could not result in pregnancy.

The cycle of a woman's fertility was only discovered in modern times in the 1920s. Here is an example of God's knowledge and wisdom at work thousands of years before men came to the same conclusions.

5. Regulations regarding polygamy: A man was allowed to have more than one wife. However, none of his wives were to be closely related to one another.
6. Regulations regarding business dealings.
7. Regulations regarding the Sabbath year: The fields were to be left uncultivated every seventh year.
8. Regulations regarding the quarantine and cleansing of leprosy: Here, too, we find

The Ten Commandments

There was a man in China who lived from 551–479 B.C. named Confucius. He taught a very similar moral law to the one given to Moses. This proves what the Apostle Paul says in his letter to the Romans: *"When Gentiles [non-Jewish people], who do not have the law [of Moses], by nature do the things in the law... are a law to themselves. [They] show the work of the law written in their hearts, their conscience also bearing witness, and between themselves their thoughts [lead to] accusing or else excusing them. [This will be revealed] in the day when God will judge the secrets of men by Jesus Christ"* (Romans 2:14–16).

another example of God's knowledge and wisdom. He knew how to limit infectious diseases long before modern man arrived at the same precautions.
9. Regulations regarding the three annual feasts of Passover, Harvest, and Ingathering.

This covenant or treaty between God and Israel was made legal through an animal blood sacrifice.

Then God made a statement which proves a part of the Trinity of the Godhead in Exodus 23:20–23. He declares that He is sending an "Angel" before Israel, and that Yahweh's name is in this Angel. That means, he has the same name as the Father Yahweh, because this Angel is the Son Yahweh. About 1,500 years later, He came down to Earth and assumed a human body through the virgin birth. He received the name Jesus, which means "Saviour." He is just as much God as his Father Yahweh.

22.

Israel's Disobedience

As I said, the people could not stand to hear God speak to them loudly, and therefore they asked Moses to speak to them on His behalf. So God called Moses up onto the mountain. He stayed there for forty days. This seemed unduly long for the people. They wondered what had happened to him. In their insecurity and unbelief, in spite of the visible proofs of God's presence, they forgot all that God had spoken to them, and they fell back into idol worship.

They had a golden calf made to be their god, and they wanted to go back to Egypt. God told Moses what was happening in the camp below. When Moses came down from the mountain, his face shone, a reflection of God's Glory. The people could not look upon his face. He had to cover it with a veil until that glow faded away. Moses was so angry about Israel's departure from God that he smashed the two tablets to pieces. He destroyed the golden calf and punished the people severely. After that, he went back up on the mountain. God threatened to annihilate Israel and offered to begin a new nation through Moses, but Moses pleaded with God not to do so.

Here the character of Moses really became evident. He would have rather that God destroy him and let the people of Israel live. He reminded God of His promises to the patriarchs of Israel, and God in His mercy listened to Moses and relented. Moses had to cut new stone tablets, bring them to God, and again God wrote His commandments on them. Moses asked God, out of his heart's despair, *"Please show me Your glory"* (Exodus 33:18). God was gracious enough to let that happen to comfort him.

God ordered Moses to build a container for the stone tablets called the "Ark of the Covenant," and to place them in it. He also ordered Israel to build in the desert a tent temple called the Tabernacle. It was divided into a Holy and a Most Holy room. In this latter room, the ark was to

The Redemption Story

be set down. God promised to be present in this inner room and talk to Moses from it.

God also ordained Moses' brother Aaron to be the High Priest of Israel. His job was to intercede for Israel with animal sacrifices to gain forgiveness for their sins. It is an eternal, divine truth that *"without shedding of blood there is no remission [of sins]"* (Hebrews 9:22). God told Israel through Moses, *"See, I have set before you today life and good, death and evil... therefore choose life, that both you and your descendants may live"* (Deuteronomy 30:15,19).

The history of Israel is a tragic report of how Israel failed God again and again. They continued to do this even after their King Solomon built the first temple for God in Jerusalem, in which God made Himself present. They could not let go of following idols. Finally, they grew to become even worse than the heathen peoples that God had destroyed by the hands of Israel. Needing to be fair, God was left with no choice. He had to punish Israel in a similar fashion. But first God sent to them His prophets, *"rising up early and sending them"* (Jeremiah 26:5).

These prophets were some of God's faithful men and women. God revealed Himself to them. He equipped them with the Holy Spirit and sent them to warn Israel of the dire consequences of not ridding themselves of their idols and worshipping Yahweh alone. He warned them that He would have to destroy them just as he had the heathen peoples before them. He told them that He would have their temple destroyed and the people sent into captivity. However, He would save a remnant of the people, because of the promises made to their patriarchs, Abraham and Jacob.

God foretold through these prophets the coming of the Saviour. He would give them a new covenant for the faithful. However, Israel by and large did not listen to God's messengers, and so the judgments of God followed. The foretellings of the prophets Isaiah, Daniel, and Zechariah are especially amazing, and 80% are alleged to have been fulfilled up to our time. No other religious book in the world can claim such a feat. This is one of the proofs of the truth of Yahweh God and His Word, the Bible.

After many warnings, God finally let the kings of Assyria (722 B.C.) and Babylon (587 B.C.) sweep in and take Israel captive. In Babylon, they had to remain in exile for seventy years, according to God's order. Thereafter, King Cyrus of Medo-Persia, whose birth was foretold 150 years before by the prophet Isaiah, was ordered by God to set Israel free. He did so in 538 B.C. and ordered the rebuilding of the city of Jerusalem and its second temple.

The returning Jews were once and for all cured of idol worship. They had been a nation of at least five million people before, but now only about sixty thousand of them returned in freedom to the land of Israel. However, they fell into another trap: that of Jewish formalism, which Jesus in His time had a lot of trouble with. The Jewish sects of the Pharisees and the Sadducees came into existence and dominated Israel's religious and political life. They added to God's laws many hard to keep details, causing a lot of Jewish people to become hypocrites in the exercise of their religion.

23.

PARTICULARS OF PROPHECIES REGARDING THE SON OF GOD, THE SAVIOUR JESUS CHRIST

Earlier I established that the theme of the Old Testament is "God's preparations for mankind's redemption." The Old Testament proves that no person can achieve eternal happiness and redemption from his or her burdens of sin through any self efforts. Actually, the Bible comes to the following conclusions: *"All have sinned and fall short of the glory of God"* (Romans 3:23). Job says, *"How then can man be righteous before God? Or how can he be pure who is born of a woman?"* (Job 25:4). David says, *"In sin my mother conceived me"* (Psalm 51:5). In Psalm 49, the sons of Korah say: *"Hear this, all peoples; give ear, all inhabitants of the world, both low and high, rich and poor... None of [you] can by any means redeem [your] brother, nor give to God a ransom for [yourself]—for the redemption of [your] souls is costly, and it shall cease forever—that [you] should continue to live eternally, and not [experience corruption]"* (Psalm 49:1–2,7–9).

It took God Himself to break that cycle of sin and death in that He sent His Son Yahweh, our Saviour Jesus Christ, down to earth to produce redemption for mankind. It cost the life of Jesus. We find the first prophecy of Him coming on a future day in Genesis 3:15 (4000 B.C.), when God promised the coming of not a man's, but a "Woman's Seed." In Genesis 15 (2000 B.C.), He is the seed of a virgin coming from Abraham's descendants. In Genesis 49, Jacob (1700 B.C.) calls Him "Shiloh," meaning "Rest" or "Messiah," the "Anointed King" coming from the tribe of Judah. Moses (1500 B.C.) says, *"The Lord your God will raise up for you a Prophet like me from your midst, from your brethren. Him you shall hear"* (Deuteronomy 18:15). In 2 Samuel 7:16 (1000 B.C.), it is made clear that the Messiah will come from King David's family and reign eternally. Psalm 22 (900 B.C.) speaks of His sufferings, even of His crucifixion and the soldiers dividing His garments among themselves and casting lots for some of them. Even the words of Jesus on the cross are forecast in the first verse: *"My God, My God, why have You forsaken Me?"* (Psalm 22:1).

The Prophet Isaiah (700 B.C.) speaks of His virgin birth in Chapter 7, and in Chapter 9 he says the words that are often read at Christmas: *"For unto us a Child is born, unto us a Son is given; and the government will be on His shoulder. And His name will be called Wonderful, Counselor, Mighty God, Everlasting Father, [and] Prince of Peace"* (Isaiah 9:6). In Chapter 11, He is called a Branch of David's family, filled with the Holy Spirit and ruling the whole world. In Micah (720 B.C.) Chapter 5, His birthplace is made known: Bethlehem in Judah. In Daniel (534 B.C.) Chapter 9, His birth date and death date is foretold exactly to the day. In Isaiah (700 B.C.) Chapter 53, all the details of His sufferings are outlined and it is revealed that He bears all our sins, intercedes

The Redemption Story

for us, lives eternally, claims victory over death, and will have a "seed": His believers and followers. Zechariah (518 B.C.) Chapter 6 outlines His ministry. He will unite the offices of priest and king into one. The last prophet of the Old Testament, Malachi (425 B.C.), declares that a curse is pronounced on the earth if people will not repent.

This very concise presentation leaves out many more prophecies to be found in the Old Testament, but these will give you a clear picture:

1. of the predicting power of God in the Bible, and
2. of the predictions of Christ's coming, His birthday, ministry, suffering, death, resurrection, and final eternal kingship.

When was Jesus actually born? A Christian monk by the name of Dionysius Exiguus (500–545 A.D.) tried to determine the birth date of Christ. He did not have the resources we have today, so he mistakenly fixed the birthday of Jesus on December 25, in the year 753 after the founding of the city of Rome. Thus Christians celebrate Christ's birthday on that day even today. It seems useless to undertake a correction in the face of this age old tradition. The sources and tools we have today allow us to fix His real birth and death date quite accurately. He was born on March 5, 4 B.C., and died on the cross on March 27, 31 A.D., at 3:00 in the afternoon. He lived on earth to be thirty-five years and twenty-one days old.

24.

A Compact Presentation of Christ's Ministry on Earth

At this point, it should be clear what God wants of people for their own welfare, and how people continually disobeyed God, and that God finally became fed up and took matters into His own hands. He not only promised to send His own Son to create a change and a new covenant, but He actually did it. After all the prophecies about the coming Messiah, God speaks these words through the Prophet Micah: *"[God] has shown you, O man, what is good; and what does the Lord require of you but to do justly, to love mercy, and to walk humbly with your God?"* (Micah 6:8). His will is summed up by Moses: *"And now, Israel, what does the Lord your God require of you, but to [respect] the Lord your God, to walk in all His ways and to love Him, to serve the Lord your God with all your heart and with all your soul, and to keep the commandments of the Lord and His statutes which I command you today for your good?"* (Deuteronomy 10:12–13). And in Leviticus, He says: *"You shall love your neighbor as yourself"* (Leviticus 19:18).

With the Ten Commandments, God set in place the best possible law for the benefit of each individual, as well as

The Redemption Story

for all human society. Since no one ever fully kept the commandments of God, all of us—both Jews and the rest of us—have failed God. Without God's intervention, we are all sinners condemned to follow Satan, the Devil. His lot is the eternal fiery hell. All unredeemed sinners who belong to Satan will end up there unless a way out could be found. Fortunately, it has been found in the mission and the work of God's Son, Jesus Christ. God's condition to receive this redemption is very simple: Repent of your sins, accept Him as your personal Saviour and Lord, and follow His teaching.

Jesus' teaching is in agreement with God's law. Jesus said, *"'You shall love the Lord your God with all your heart, with all your soul, and with all your mind.' This is the first and great commandment. And the second is like it: 'You shall love your neighbor as yourself.'"* (Matthew 22:37–39). In other words, do unto others what you would have them do unto you.

Jesus began His ministry in Nazareth, his hometown in Israel (Matthew 2:23). There He quoted the prophet Isaiah as an outline of His ministry program: *"The Spirit of the Lord is upon me, because He has anointed Me to preach the gospel to the poor; He has sent Me to heal the brokenhearted, to proclaim liberty to the captives and recovery of sight to the blind, to set at liberty those who are oppressed, to proclaim the acceptable year of the Lord"* (Luke 4:18–19).

He was baptized (washed, immersed) by John the Baptist in the river Jordan to fulfill the wishes of His heavenly Father. John was the promised "Way Preparer." When Jesus rose out of the water, the Holy Spirit flew upon Him in bodily form the way a dove settles down into a perch. The voice of God was heard saying, *"This is My beloved Son in whom I am well pleased"* (Matthew 3:17). The Holy Spirit stayed with Jesus until His death on the cross.

Jesus' message to the people was in short: *"The kingdom of God is at hand. Repent, and believe in the gospel"* (Mark 1:15). Jesus also said, *"He who believes and is baptized will be saved"* (Mark 16:16). Baptism was to be a symbol of spiritual purification and death to the old sinful lifestyle. It was also to be a symbol of the birth of a new lifestyle in obedience toward God, making one a citizen of the Kingdom of God.

The Apostle Paul tells us that when we do what Jesus asks us to do, we become a part of the family of God Himself as His sons and daughters.

25.

SOME OF THE TEACHINGS OF JESUS

Blessed are the poor in spirit, for theirs is the kingdom of heaven.

Blessed are those who mourn, for they shall be comforted.

Blessed are the meek, for they shall inherit the earth.

Blessed are those who hunger and thirst for righteousness, for they shall be filled.

The Redemption Story

> Blessed are the merciful, for they shall obtain mercy.
>
> Blessed are the pure in heart, for they shall see God.
>
> Blessed are the peacemakers, for they shall be called [children] of God.
>
> Blessed are those who are persecuted for righteousness' sake, for theirs is the kingdom of heaven.
>
> Blessed are you when they revile and persecute you, and say all kinds of evil against you falsely for My sake. (Matthew 5:3–11)

Furthermore, He taught: *"You are the salt of the earth [to keep mankind from rotting away totally]... You are the light of the world [by your exemplary living and good works]"* (Matthew 5:13–14). Paraphrased, He also said, "Have your heart changed for the good. Live a sexually pure life. Do not worry about life's basic needs, for if you give the Kingdom of God the first place in your life, God will look after you. Do not criticize people, and leave people who reject the Good News and make fun of it alone. Do not talk about the Christian religion with them anymore, but leave them in the hands of God's judgment."

He compares the process of becoming a believer of Jesus Christ to a rebirth, having died from a sinful life and been resurrected to a blissful life. For three and a half years (27–31 A.D.), Jesus went preaching and gathering disciples (learners, students). He performed many miracles in healing the sick, raising the dead, feeding the hungry, and controlling nature. With this, He proved Himself to be more than just an ordinary man. He called Himself "the Son of Man"—indicating that He was a true man—and also "the Son of God"—indicating that He was also the true God. He predicted His suffering, crucifixion, resurrection, and return to heaven. His disciples could not understand this, because they were looking for a deliverer from the Roman yoke and the re-establishment of the kingdom of Israel.

26.

Conflict with Israel's Leaders

It is noteworthy to look at the education of Jewish children during Jesus' time, especially boys. By age ten, they had to be familiar with the five books of Moses, called the Torah. By age thirteen, they had to be familiar with the whole Old Testament, called the Tanakh by the Jews. After a test, they would be declared a "Bar Mitzvah" (in English, "Son of the Commandment").

Even Jesus went through this process (Luke 2:41–50). The poor could not afford the costs of this religious education, and because of the dominant view that females were inferior to males—a belief perpetuated especially by the

The Redemption Story

Pharisees—very few girls ever received a formal education. The Pharisees even doubted that a woman had a soul!

Jesus and his foster father Joseph were "Tektons" by trade. Many English Bibles translate this term as "carpenters." However, the proper translation today would be "construction technicians," because their main building materials were not wood, but stones, mortar, and clay. As construction technicians, they belonged not to the poor, but to the middle class in Israel. The Apostle Paul says that Jesus, though being in the form of God, made Himself of no reputable status, but took upon Himself the status of a slave (Philippians 2:5–8). He also says that Jesus Christ, though rich, yet for our sakes made himself poor (2 Corinthians 8:9). The word "rich" in this passage is not referring to earthly possessions of Jesus, but rather to His real status as the Son of God. Jesus Himself once told a would-be follower that *"foxes have holes and birds of the air have nests, but the Son of Man has nowhere to lay His head"* (Luke 9:58). He was often a guest in the Apostle Peter's home in Capernaum, as well as with a family in Bethany that consisted of the siblings Martha, Mary ("Miriam"), and Lazarus. During His three and a half years of ministry, His financial support came from a number of well-to-do women. This came about because Jesus accepted women as human beings equal with men, a belief that was in sharp contrast with that of contemporary Jewish sects.

Christ's opponents were the Pharisees and the Sadducees. The sect of the Pharisees believed that the oral traditions of Israel had more importance than the written Old Testament. The Pharisees were quite popular in Israel.

Their members included persons of all classes. Out of their teachings evolved a book called the Talmud, which is still studied today. Next to some Bible passages, it contains the opinions, teachings, and traditions as recorded by Jewish rabbis (teachers). Their religion evolved through the ages to the present Orthodox Jewish Synagogue (gathering house).

The Sadducees were strict followers of the Torah and held the temple services. They were the rich, the suppliers of High Priests and rulers in Christ's time. Some of them were rich businessmen. They did not believe in life after death or the resurrection of the dead, as the Pharisees did. Their philosophy was, "if you keep the Law of God (the Torah), you will have the best life possible on earth until you die." This is true, except:

1. No man ever could fulfill all the requirements of the law.
2. There is life after death and a coming resurrection of the dead, according to Jesus Christ Himself. And as the Son of God, He ought to know.

Every person has to appear before the final judgment of God, as described in Revelation 20:1–15. The verdict issued there will decide whether a person will live eternally in heaven (John 3:16) or in the eternal hell called "Gehenna" (Revelation 19:20 and 21:8).

Jesus accepted the entire Old Testament as God's Word. He repeatedly quoted from it. He said, *"For assuredly, I say to you, till heaven and earth pass away, one jot or one tittle will by no means pass from the law till all is fulfilled"* (Matthew 5:18). By this stand, it is clear that He would come into conflict with the two sects and rulers of Israel.

27.
THE CONFLICT ISSUES

The conflict began with Christ's cleansing of the temple in Jerusalem.

King Solomon had built the first temple dedicated to the worship of Yahweh. This temple was destroyed by the Babylonian king Nebuchadnezzar in 587 B.C. God had foretold that He would have this temple destroyed, because of Israel's unrepentant sins against Him. About fifty-one years later, King Cyrus came to power. Some Jewish scholars informed the king of the prophecies of him in the book of Isaiah (44:24–28). These prophecies had been given about 150 years before King Cyrus' birth. Israel had fulfilled the foretold seventy-year captivity (Jeremiah 25:1–14), and the time had come for them to return to Palestine.

King Cyrus of Medo-Persia (today's Iran) issued a proclamation for the Jews to return to their homeland. Only about sixty thousand actually returned. They rebuilt Jerusalem, and built the second temple during seven years between 538–516 B.C. Other Jews decided to remain in Medo-Persia, for they had taken root there. They began to have their religious meetings in houses called synagogues, meaning "gathering houses." From these, the office of the Rabbi (teacher) arose. The second temple was expensively renovated and decorated by King Herod the Great, beginning in 20 B.C. Work was still being done to it when Jesus was thirty-three years old.

The conflict issues between Jesus and the leaders of Israel were:

1. The Sadducees had permitted their business colleagues to conduct business on temple grounds. They sold animals dedicated for sacrifices and exchanged currency. In other words, the Sadducees had essentially changed the House of Prayer into a business mall. This raised the ire of Jesus Christ. He made Himself a whip of cords and drove them all out of the temple grounds shouting, *"Take these things away! Do not make My Father's house a house of merchandise!"* (John 2:16). The Sadducees became angry. At the close of His ministry, Jesus repeated the same action, which brought about the decision of the Sadducees to kill Him.

2. A second reason for seeking to kill Jesus was that He claimed to be the Son of God, *"making Himself equal with God"* (John 5:18). They considered this a blasphemy. They were blind to the Old Testament appearances of and prophecies about Jesus Christ. It never dawned on them that God was more than one person, the Father, but that He also included the Holy Spirit and the Son of God in the Godhead.

3. The third reason for seeking to kill Jesus was His criticism of the hypocrisy of the Jewish leaders.

4. The fourth reason was the raising of Lazarus from the dead. This and many other miracles Jesus performed caused

a lot of people to believe in Him. They called Him "Rabbi" and wondered if Jesus might be the Bible's promised Messiah, who would renew the kingdom of Israel. This, in turn, caused the jealousy of the Pharisees and they exclaimed: *"Look, the world has gone after Him!"* (John 12:19)

5. The fifth reason was that some Jewish people wanted to make Jesus king, after He had fed thousands of them miraculously. This got the Jewish leaders really excited. They feared trouble with the representatives of the Roman Empire who had occupied Israel since 63 B.C.

Thus, the stage for the execution of Jesus Christ was set.

28.

THE PASSION OF JESUS CHRIST

Because of His teaching and ministry of love, Jesus became very popular among the Jewish people. However, the leadership saw in Him a great threat. Therefore the otherwise opposing groups of Pharisees and Sadducees set their conflicts aside and united themselves to get rid of Jesus. They wanted to proceed carefully so as not to cause an uproar among the people, and they wanted to do it fast enough that the people wouldn't have a chance to rebel against their plan. So they waited for an opportunity to arrest Him without disturbing the public.

This opportunity came when one of his twelve disciples, Judas of Iscariot, decided to betray Jesus at the time of the Passover feast in the Spring of 31 A.D. Why he did that is a mystery, except that he was pushed into this despicable act by Satan. It appears to me that Judas had wanted to force Jesus to use His divine powers politically against the Jewish and Roman authorities. He probably hoped that Jesus would declare a free and divine kingdom of Israel.

Jesus, however, was aware of what was going on in Judas' mind. At the Passover meal, which was eaten at night, Jesus said to His disciples, *"One of you will betray Me"* (John 13:21). When John the son of Zebedee quietly asked Jesus who that person would be, Jesus indicated that it was Judas. During the meal, Jesus told Judas, *"What you do, do quickly"* (John 13:27).

During his three and a half years of ministry, Jesus had foretold several times that the Jewish authorities would eventually have him crucified, but that he would rise from the dead on the third day. Now the time for this drama had come.

Judas went to the high priests. They gave him thirty silver coins for his services, and Judas led a group of temple guards and royal soldiers to arrest Jesus.

In the meantime, Jesus and His disciples went to a garden called Gethsemane, a favourite place of Jesus'. In that garden, He battled with Himself in prayer for courage to go through all the things He knew awaited Him. In His agony, He sweated profusely. Finally, He overcame Himself and committed Himself to do His Father's will. He would become the atonement for our sins, yours and mine included,

The Redemption Story

and die willingly on the cross for us. Angels appeared and comforted Him.

Jesus was arrested and brought before the high priests. False witnesses stood up against Him, but failed. Finally, the high priest Caiaphas put Jesus under oath to ask Him whether He was the "Son of God." Jesus declared that he was. Hearing this, the high priests pronounced the death penalty upon Jesus for "blasphemy." Since the Jews were not allowed to execute anyone on their own, they took Jesus to the Roman governor Pontius Pilatus.

First, Pilate did not want to have anything to do with Jesus. Only when they accused Jesus, claiming He had declared Himself the king of the Jews, did Pilate see himself forced to act, though He did realize that the charge was phoney. However, after some futile attempts to free, he commanded Jesus to be crucified.

The process was a gruesome one. First there came whippings and beatings so that Jesus' body was completely bloodied. Then followed the crucifixion itself, when the Romans pounded spikes through Jesus' wrists and feet, affixing him to the cross. Here the prophecy of Isaiah, given some seven hundred years before, were finally fulfilled in detail (see Isaiah 53:1–12).

Jesus went through all this so that you and I need not go to hell. He wants us to enjoy a happy eternal life. The only condition is that we ask Him to forgive us our sins, trust in Him, and follow His and His apostles' teachings in the New Testament.

29.

THE RESURRECTION OF JESUS CHRIST

It has been said that if someone does not know about the resurrection of Jesus Christ, he or she is in the dark regarding the most important event of all world history.

In modern times, there has been an ongoing discussion regarding the legitimacy of the story of Jesus Christ's resurrection. However, hardly any historical event has produced so many comments. There are thousands of ancient copies that deal with this event, which goes to show its importance to the human experience.

There is the story, popular among Muslims, that Jesus never died on the cross at all, but that He came to himself, escaped from the tomb, and ended up in India where He married and had children. At a certain town, there is a gravestone with the name of "Jesus" written on it, seeming to prove this theory.

1. The truth of the matter is that the name Jesus (Jeshuah, in Hebrew) was a common name among the Jews. Jews still live in parts of India, Pakistan, and Nepal to this day.

The Redemption Story

There may have been thousands of Jeshuahs living in Jesus' time.
2. It is impossible for anyone to recover from a crucifixion ordeal and still have enough strength to move a one ton stone door back in its track to escape from such a tomb, especially from the inside.

Another theory is that the disciples overwhelmed the Roman guards watching Jesus' grave (four soldiers at a time, changing every three hours), took Jesus out of the tomb, and revived Him. This is what the leaders of the Jews expected, as recorded in Matthew 27:62–66. If that really would have happened, though, we can be sure that the Roman and Jewish authorities would have hunted the disciples down and killed them. That would have been the end of the Christian Church.

A third modern theory is expressed in the book *The Passover Plot*, by Hugh J. Schonfield, which proposes that Jesus and His disciples devised the plan to have Jesus crucified, and then to save him before He died, ushering him out of public view, and spreading the resurrection story for religious and political reasons.

Then Dan Brown disbursed the silly notion in *The Da Vinci Code* that Jesus was married to Mary Magdalene, who was pregnant with His child. Brown's book postulates that she escaped to France after Jesus' death, where she became absorbed in the Merovingian dynasty of kings, so that there is still a descendant of Jesus living today. The whole story has been exposed as a fraud.

The fact remains that more than six thousand persons who wrote the ancient letters were convinced of Jesus' resurrection. The Apostle Paul says in 1 Corinthians 15 that on one of the many occasions Jesus showed Himself alive after His death by crucifixion, He was seen by five hundred "brethren" at once. That term "brethren" means "males," females not being mentioned. He also says that at the point of writing this, many of those witnesses were still living. They could have contradicted him. No one ever did.

How did the resurrection of Jesus happen? Our best witness is the Apostle John, the youngest of Christ's disciples. He had a special place in the heart of Jesus, because of his youth. He was the only male disciple who stood by the cross. He watched all the proceedings, together with some female disciples, the mother of Jesus, Mary the wife of Clopas, and Mary Magdalene. Luke writes that *all* of His acquaintances watched these things unfold at a distance (Luke 23:49). John documented for us that Jesus indeed truly died. He watched a Roman soldier stick his spear into His heart, to see if He was indeed dead. Blood and water came out of this wound. Such a thing only happens when a person has died and the red blood cells separate themselves from the white or clear cells. This proves that death has taken place.

At burial, Jesus' body was first washed with water. Thereafter, it was wrapped in a linen bandage similar to the Egyptian mummies. On Easter morning, an angel appeared at the grave site. This shocked the Roman soldiers so much that they first fell down as though dead, and then ran away from the grave. He rolled away the big stone wheel which served as a door (a common sighting in Jerusalem in ancient

The Redemption Story

days). He exposed the empty tomb. Jesus appeared first to Mary Magdalene. Her report to the disciples was disbelieved, though Peter and John ran to see what had happened at the grave. John went into the open grave and saw the linen wrapping flattened. They did not contain a body anymore. How could the body of Jesus have escaped from its covering without it being unwound? Impossible!

Therefore John began to believe Mary Magdalene, and the rest of the disciples wondered what had happened.

Then Jesus appeared to them alive at evening time, when they were still together, fearful of the reaction of the Jewish authorities. He suddenly appeared in the middle of the room while the door was locked, and greeted them with the usual Jewish greeting, "Shalom!" ("Peace!") After this, He appeared to them together and also individually. He explained to them the Old Testament prophecies concerning Himself that had to be fulfilled.

To ascertain the reality of Jesus' resurrection, like in a court case, there has to be some proofs, such as firsthand witness reports, direct evidences, and circumstantial (indirect) evidences.

1. The firsthand witness reports come to us in the form of the ancient writings, especially the three Gospels by Matthew, Mark, and John, who were all eyewitnesses of Jesus' life and ministry. The scriptural law states, "Every word shall be established upon two or three witnesses" (Deuteronomy 17:6, Matthew 18:16). That condition is clearly met.

2. In the way of direct evidence, we have the Shroud of Turin, which shows the image of a crucified man imprinted into the cloth. What is the Turin shroud? It is an ancient piece of cloth. Such shrouds were used by the Jews, who laid linen-wrapped corpses upon them and rolled them over the feet right up to the head. An additional small piece of cloth, the face cloth, was laid upon the corpse's face. This particular face cloth also exists, in Spain. It is claimed that the image in the shroud is a photo negative imprint of the crucified Jesus Christ. There has been an ongoing battle between believers and sceptic scientists who deny that the image is a true photo negative. Other scientists declare there are undeniable proofs that the image on the cloth is indeed a photographic image of the crucified Jesus Christ.

At present, the weight of evidence overrules the view of the sceptics. Some of the evidential points are: a) The age of the cloth is right. b) The weaving style is right. c) Plant pollen found on the cloth prove that the shroud originates from the area of Jerusalem. d) Blood samples taken from the bloody stains of the shroud classify the blood group AB, prevalent in the Middle East and southern Europe.

The Wyatt Archaeological Research Centre claims to have found the Jewish Ark of the Covenant. It is supposed to be located in a cave that is situated directly below the crucifixion site of Jesus Christ. Some of His blood has apparently seeped through the cracks of the rock on top of the ark. If this is the case, and blood samples can be obtained and compared with the samples from the Turin shroud, showing that the two samples are identical and there is a DNA match, absolute scientific proof not only of Jesus Christ's crucifixion, but also His resurrection, may soon be revealed.

The Redemption Story

Why is this proof of the resurrection, you ask? The reason is that, in Christ's day, there was no such thing as a manmade camera. So how did the image get into the cloth? It can only have been caused by the supernatural light that filled the grave chamber at the moment of Christ's resurrection, which burned a photo negative into the cloth.

3. Circumstantial evidence arises from realistic practical experiences with the living Christ. There are also some of these available. For one, there is the story of Betty Baxter, from Fairmont, Minnesota. Jesus appeared to the hopelessly crippled girl, who doctors said could only live to be fifteen years of age, and healed her completely. The story became famous. Betty became a beautiful, normal woman. She felt called to the ministry as a Pentecostal evangelist, and never married, because there was no greater love in her life than Jesus.

A second witness of the living Christ's presence is Alec Moishe Weinberger, a Jew who survived the holocaust in Nazi Germany. After a terribly unsteady life, including crimes and drugs, he was saved from his life of sin by the personal appearance of Jesus Christ, who called him by the name his mother had used for him in his childhood: "Moishela!" He describes Jesus this way: "He was tall... I can only describe Him as beautiful. He had dark eyebrows and the most wonderful blue eyes I had ever seen. They were full of light and piercing right into me. His hair was snow white and fell on His shoulders. He had a full, white beard to His waist. His robe was purple, edged in gold, opening down the front like an undershirt. Around His waist was a gold sash. As I gazed, speechless, He spoke, again in Hebrew."[13]

I consider my own testimony to stand witness to the living Christ. Though I never saw Jesus in the flesh, He has spoken to me twice. The first time, I heard Him as a voice within myself. The second time, He called me by name, quite loudly, three times one night, awaking me from sleep. My wife was also a witness to this. At that point, He gave me a ministry. I did not want to obey, but finally, while the morning sun came up, I agreed to take it upon myself. Many years later, He took me up to heaven for a few minutes, on Sunday, June 28, 1998. I did not want to come back to this life on earth, because it was so beautiful and peaceful there.

Jesus came to die on the cross for our sins. He is giving us a chance to receive forgiveness from Him and be set free from the judgment of God. Once again, His only condition is that we accept Him as our Saviour and Lord for life and follow His teachings. These teachings make sense and are wholesome for us, both personally and in the lives of people we touch on a daily basis. From the moment we ask for His forgiveness and accept Him and trust Him, He grants us eternal life together with Him in heaven. There will be no more sorrow, sickness, and death. He has promised to be with us every day of our life (Matthew 28:20). He will teach us and guide us through His Holy Spirit (John 14:26). This is why I invite you to take these steps, join an Evan-

---

[13] Weinberger, A.M. *I Escaped the Holocaust*. Beaverlodge: Horizon House Publishers (1978), p. 69.

gelical Christian Church, and work along with that congregation until the Lord Jesus takes you home to heaven.

30.

HOW THE CHRISTIAN CHURCH CAME TO BE

How did the Christian Church come into existence? Most churches teach that the Church started at Pentecost, but that is a mistake. A prophecy in the Old Testament tells us who built the Church, and when. It is found in the writings of the Prophet Zechariah, where it says, *"Behold, the Man whose name is the BRANCH! From His place He shall branch out, and <u>He shall build the temple of the Lord</u>; Yes, He shall build the temple of the Lord. He shall bear the glory, and shall sit and rule on His throne; so He shall be a priest on His throne, and the counsel of peace shall be between them both"* (Zechariah 6:12–13, emphasis mine).

1. This name, "the Branch," is a name of Jesus Christ, because He is a branch of the "trunk" (family) of King David, according to the Prophet Isaiah (11:1).
2. As the text in Zechariah hints, Jesus branched out from His place, which was Nazareth in Galilee.

3. He built the new temple of God, a spiritual living temple consisting of all born again Christians (1 Corinthians 3:16–17, 6:19, and 2 Corinthians 6:16).
4. After that, He was glorified by His sacrificial love at Calvary, was resurrected from the dead, and ascended to the throne of God in heaven.
5. Sitting on His throne, He united the offices of King and Priest into one; that is, into Himself.

Since this new temple consists of people likened as "living stones" by the Apostle Peter (1 Peter 2:5), when did He do it? Jesus began to do it when He gathered disciples (students) around Himself. Some pastors claim that He succeeded in winning only twelve believers during His ministry on earth: His twelve disciples. That is wrong. The Bible clearly teaches in 1 Corinthians 15:6 that Christ was seen after His resurrection by over five hundred brethren at one time. This happened before the event of Pentecost. One can safely assume that most of these five hundred brethren were married and also had children. This makes a church at least two thousand persons strong before Pentecost. These people were born again before Pentecost by receiving the Holy Spirit on Easter Sunday evening. Jesus appeared to His disciples, blew at them, and said; "Receive the Holy Spirit." Also, before Pentecost, this church had a business meeting. About 120 believers were present, as recorded in Acts 1:15.

The Redemption Story

So what was the event of Pentecost for? Jesus explained this in Acts 1:8. *"You shall receive power."* The Greek word Jesus used for "power" is *dunamin,* meaning "authority". From this word, we have the English word "dynamite." Christians were to have the authority and boldness to witness about Jesus Christ to the whole world. The word "witness" in the Greek language is *martus*, which also encompasses the meaning of "martyrs." In other words, Christians would receive so much spiritual power that they could spread the word about Jesus with authority and have enough courage to do it under the threat of martyrdom. This still happens today. What a contrast this is to the days when the disciples met behind locked doors for fear of the Jews! (John 20:19) To this church were *added,* the Bible says, three thousand souls at Pentecost (Acts 2:41).

Someone once compared the mission of Christ to the building of the first temple under King Solomon. In the same way that King David collected building materials for this temple, so did John the Baptist collect believers for Christ's new spiritual temple. Just as King Solomon Jedidiah built the first temple with earthly material, Jesus Christ builds His spiritual temple with born again believers. As God's glory came upon the first temple to dedicate and empower it (2 Chronicles 7:1), God's Presence moved inside this new spiritual temple on the day of Pentecost (Acts 2:1–4). The Holy Spirit came, dedicated and empowered the spiritual temple—the Church—where God's Presence dwells today. The likeness between the two temples is even more relevant by noting that the name Solomon means "Man of peace," and his surname Jedidiah means "Beloved of Yahweh." Jesus, the Saviour, is our Man of peace. He is also the "Beloved Son of God" (Matthew 3:17).

31.

THE HAPPENINGS AT THE FEAST OF PENTECOST

The record of the story of Pentecost is found in Acts 2. A lot of people say that there were 120 disciples in the upper room. That, however, is not correct. These 120 persons were present for the business meeting mentioned in Acts 1. The actual number of people gathered together on the day of Pentecost is not mentioned. The words "all together" does not reflect merely the 120, but rather everybody who was present at this occasion. The upper room was probably located in the home of John Mark's mother, one of the financial supporters of the Lord Jesus. This home appears to have been located at a city square, because of the thousands of people who gathered before the house and heard and saw what happened to the Christians. There was only one square in old Jerusalem that fits the occasion, and it is located at the front of the temple grounds, where it still is today. The Christians were gathered together in prayer, waiting for the promise of receiving power from heaven, as the Lord Jesus had instructed them.

The Redemption Story

Suddenly there came a sound from heaven like a strong rushing wind. It filled the whole house where they were sitting. Then, there appeared to them tongues of fire, which came to rest upon every one of them. The Bible says that *"they were all filled with the Holy Spirit"* (Acts 2:4). After this, they began to speak with other "tongues" (languages). The impression the text gives is that all the disciples spoke loudly at the same time, probably in prayer worshipping God.

A lot of Christians today would say that this sounds like a lot of disorder and confusion. They are not alone in thinking this; the masses on the square thought so, too. That is why they were "amazed" and "marvelled" (Acts 2:6–7). Some had their fun, saying, "O well, they are all drunk!" Others claimed to understand what the Christians were saying. Fifteen different languages are mentioned in the text. The people said that the disciples were proclaiming the wonderful works of God in their own national languages. That is worship!

Seeing that the confused masses were not understanding this miracle, the Apostle Peter stood up and explained what was happening. He told them that it was the fulfillment of an Old Testament prophecy found in Joel 2. A key point in this prophecy is that men and women were treated equally as messengers of the Lord Jesus Christ. Both sexes were prophesying—that is, speaking or preaching in behalf of God. A lot of present day churches still do not allow women to preach, based on a statement made by the Apostle Paul in 1 Corinthians 14:34–35. They do not notice that they create a contradiction by making this claim; since there are no contradictions in the original text, this view is not biblical. God does not contradict Himself. They do not notice that Paul, in the same letter, speaks of women who prophecy, speaking on behalf of God (1 Corinthians 11:5). In Romans 16, Paul names women who have laboured in the Lord: Priscilla, Tryphena, Tryphosa (probably twins), and Persis. They are on the same level as Aquila, Philologus, and Olympas, who were either pastors or evangelists. The problem with women that Paul refers to in 1 Corinthians 11:1 and 1 Timothy 2:12 stems from the Jewish synagogue system, which had been assumed by the Jewish Christians: Men were sitting in the centre of the assembly hall, and the women were sitting along the walls. When the wives did not understand the speaker correctly, they would disturb the service, calling loudly to their husbands asking for explanations or lecturing their husbands. This, Paul forbade. In many Jewish Orthodox synagogues, you will find the same seating arrangement as in ancient times.

Back to Pentecost. Peter gave a very good message, stressing that everybody should receive the Lord Jesus Christ into their hearts to be saved. They would receive the same gift of the Holy Spirit that the disciples just received. He emphasized that this Spirit-filling program of God was not limited to his time, as a lot of churches today claim. This promise was to the firsthand listeners, as well as to *"your children, and to all that are afar off [by birth], as many as the Lord will call"* (Acts 2:39). That includes you and me.

This experience, called the baptism in the Holy Spirit, is still experienced in many churches, but mostly in Pentecostal and Charismatic circles. Baptism in the Holy Spirit is a part of what is called the Full Gospel. This means that nothing the New Testament teaches is left out of a church's statement of faith.

32.

Things that Happened After Pentecost

Though most copies of the New Testament refer to the "Book of Acts," its title could just as well be "The Acts of the Risen Christ Through His Apostles." The church grew quickly in Jerusalem through the ministry of the Apostles, both through preaching as well through performing miracles. As was the case with the ministry of Jesus, this did not escape the attention of the authorities. They arrested Peter and John, but could not agree about what to do to them, so they let them go after forbidding them to preach about Jesus Christ. Naturally, the disciples did not obey that command, replying: *"Whether it is right in the sight of God to listen to you more than to God, you judge. For we cannot but speak the things which we have seen and heard"* (Acts 4:19–20).

There was such an enthusiasm among believers that they sold their property and lived together and held things in common. This system of society is still practiced today by the Hutterites and other similar groups. For the early church, however, it did not work out too well over time. Eventually, they became impoverished and had to be supported by other churches that came to exist through the later ministry of the Apostle Paul (2 Corinthians 8:16–22). The other churches that came into existence through the work of the apostles operated in a similar fashion to the churches today.

The first problem in the Jerusalem church was twofold:

1. The overburdening of the Apostles by them having to both prepare for preaching and properly look after the needs of the widows of their church, at the same time.
2. The accusation was brought forward that the Apostles favoured the local widows over widows who came from other countries and ended up in the Jerusalem church speaking Greek rather than Aramaic.

To manage this overburdening, they selected seven trustworthy men to serve "the tables" (look after the food requirements) of these people in the church. They were called "deacons," meaning "servants." The organization of the early church followed the Jewish synagogue system, which is not surprising considering that all of these people were Jewish.

They had an administrator, called a "bishop," to oversee the administration of the group. A bishop in the early church may also have been responsible for the treasury of the congregation. So bishops and deacons were, in fact, organizational servants, or "business elders" of a congregation.

The Redemption Story

Beyond these roles, the church had pastors ("shepherds"), preachers/ teachers, evangelists, and prophets serving as "spiritual elders" (Ephesians 4:11). The pastors' job was to hold the congregations together and provide counselling for peace and spiritual development. The preacher/teachers proclaimed the Word of God from their Bibles, which basically consisted of the Old Testament and the new writings of the Apostles as they came about.

It's important to note here that not every Christian owned a Bible. Since they were all handwritten, Bibles were very expensive. Many churches did not even own all the Old Testament scriptures. Indeed, many congregations appear to have been quite small. It appears that they at times traded the scriptures amongst themselves, as hinted at in Paul's letter to the Colossians (Colossians 4:16). Therefore, the main teachers of Jesus Christ's ideas were the "Apostles," who usually traveled from church to church to give them Christian instruction, especially to the leaders. This office had been installed by Jesus Christ Himself (Luke 6:13). The word "apostle" means "One sent forth." That is why an apostle is to go "forth"—to establish churches and then revisit them for instructional purposes.

The Lord Jesus equipped them with the power to preach, heal the sick, cleanse the lepers, raise the dead, and cast out evil spirits. Further proofs of an apostleship, or "signs" of this office, were teaching by biblical knowledge and inspiration of the Holy Spirit (John 14:26), and having power for *"signs and wonders and mighty [supernatural] deeds"* (2 Corinthians 12:12). Very powerful people indeed!

The next office was that of the evangelist. These were traveling people, specialists in proclaiming the "Evangel"—that is, the Good News about Jesus Christ to people who were ignorant of the Gospel—to win them for Christ. They would at any location stay only as long as people were responding to their message. After that, they would travel on.

Finally, there was the office of the New Testament prophet. His job was to encourage people in their faith. At times, they would demonstrate a supernatural knowledge of unseen present realities or future events, as for example the prophet Agabus did (Acts 11:28).

Do we have Apostles today? Some churches say they were only given to the early church, because the canon (official list) of the New Testament books was not yet established. However, once in a while they still appear today. There was, for example, a Pentecostal preacher named Smith Wigglesworth. Originally a simple plumber, under his ministry two people were raised from the dead. Because of his fame, he is called "The Apostle of Faith." In Germany, there was the Evangelical Lutheran pastor Johann Christoph Blumhardt, under whose ministry one woman was raised from the dead. And there were—and still are—a few more.

In summary, the offices of the church were: Apostles, Bishops, Deacons, Pastors, Preachers/Teachers, Evangelists, and Prophets (Ephesians 4:11). Often the callings of a person are a combination of some of these separate offices. For example, a pastor is usually both a preacher and a teacher at the same time.

33.
THE PROGRESS OF THE EARLY CHURCH

The Church grew fast following the feast of Pentecost. Now, you might be asking, what *is* Pentecost? It is one of the three major feasts God gave Israel to celebrate. The word "Pentecost" means "fiftieth," because it is to be celebrated on the fiftieth day after the Passover feast. It is also called the "Feast of Harvest" and the "Day of the First Fruits." The product of the harvest was not to be enjoyed before an offering of it was first brought to God in the temple. In a sense, the three thousand persons who were added to the Church that day can be thought of as the "first fruits" of the Church age, also called "The Age of Grace," because God extends His grace to all nations from that day forward.

The Jewish government's fear of the tremendous growth of the Church during the years that followed caused them to begin a persecution of the Christians. The first Christian martyr was Stephen, a deacon. The sermon he preached (Acts 7) is a compact summary of the failures of Old Testament Israel, and it was the cause for his martyrdom. Then, King Herod killed James, the brother of John (the sons of Zebedee). He wanted to kill Peter also, but an angel led Peter out of the prison at night, past all the guards, so that he escaped. A Pharisee named Saul of Tarsus was then given authority from the Jewish leadership to hunt Christians down wherever they could be found. Still, the Church was all Jewish and continued to grow. They gathered for worship in private homes. On occasion, they would take over a synagogue.

Because of the persecution, the Church in Jerusalem was decimated, not only by imprisonment and killings, but also because some Christians fled to the Province of Samaria. They proclaimed Christ to the people there. Among them was Philip the deacon. A great number of people accepted the Lord Jesus Christ and were also baptized in the Holy Spirit. Philip also preached Christ to a high Ethiopian official who had been in Jerusalem for worship. From this man began the Ethiopian, or "Coptic," Church of Ethiopia and Egypt.

One day, Saul of Tarsus was on his way to arrest a group of Christians in the city of Damascus in Syria. Suddenly, a heavenly light engulfed him and the Lord Jesus Christ spoke to him, telling him to go into the city where he would be informed of what he must do. In Damascus, a Christian named Ananias was told by the Lord to meet Saul. Saul accepted the Lord Jesus as his personal Saviour and Lord and was baptized. Henceforth, Saul was known as Paulus the Apostle.

In the meantime, the Apostle Peter was summoned by God to visit a Roman captain of the Italian Regiment named Cornelius. Peter was to tell him the Good News about the Lord Jesus Christ. Since Cornelius was not Jewish, Peter had hang-ups and had to be convinced by God

The Redemption Story

that this is what He wanted. While he preached Christ to Cornelius and his household, the Holy Spirit fell on all of them just like on the Jews at Pentecost. This became an eye-opener for the Jewish Christian community that God wanted the Gospel preached to all nations, just as the Lord Jesus Himself had commanded the disciples before returning to heaven.

    The Roman Catholic Church maintains that the Church was to be built by Peter, and that Peter was its first pope. This contention, however, is a serious error, for the rest of the Apostles had received the same "keys of the Kingdom of God" (Matthew 18:18, John 20:23) that Peter did (Matthew 16:18–19). Also, Paul figures prominently in the Book of Acts. In the teaching section of the New Testament, seventeen letters were written by Paul, while Peter is represented by only two letters. Furthermore, after the first universal Church Council at Jerusalem (held before 41 A.D.), Peter is not anymore mentioned in the Book of Acts. James appears to have been the chairperson of that meeting, and Paul's theology prevailed and was accepted by the majority. Also, while popes are not to be married according to Roman Catholic doctrine, Peter was a married man (Matthew 8:14). Peter also acknowledged Paul as being superior in theological teaching (2 Peter 3:15–17). Paul formulated the first "Christian Systematic Theology" in his Letter to the Romans. From Paul's letter to the Galatians, we learn that Peter was a missionary to the Jews, while Paul was a missionary to the Gentiles (non-Jews). Paul also had to confront Peter for hypocrisy (Galatians 2:11).

Paul's missionary work spread the Christian faith from Judea to Syria, to Lebanon, to Turkey, to Greece, and then to Italy, according to the Book of Acts. Christian tradition also claims that the Apostle Paul started churches in Spain, France, and even Britain. No man in all of Christian history accomplished as much as Paul. Paul later died in Rome, beheaded by order of Emperor Nero, the madman, about 67 A.D. In fact, all Apostles of the Lord Jesus died the martyr's death, except the Apostle John, who grew to be very old and who wrote three short letters and the Book of Revelation, the last book of the New Testament.

34.

THE CHURCH UNDER THE APOSTOLIC FATHERS

When the Apostle Paul took leave from the church leaders of Ephesus, he said to them: *"Indeed, now I know that you all, among whom I have gone preaching the kingdom of God, will see my face no more. Therefore I testify to you this day that I am innocent of the blood of all people. For I have not shunned to declare to you the whole counsel of God. Therefore take heed to yourselves and to all the flock, among which the Holy Spirit has made you overseers [bishops and pastors], to shepherd the church of God which He purchased with His own blood. For I know this, that after my departure savage wolves will come in among you, not sparing the flock. Also from among yourselves men will rise up, speaking perverse things, to draw away the disciples after themselves. Therefore watch..."* (Acts 20:25–31).

This is exactly what happened. The Lord Jesus gave the Apostle John the names of some of these heretics in the Book of Revelation: A man named Nicolaus (Revelation 2:6) and a woman named Jezebel (Revelation 2:20). The teachings of the Gnostics are examples of this trend. On the one hand, the good that came out of this situation is that the orthodox churches (meaning "conforming to the teachings of the early church") pulled closer together, for each church at the beginning, after Pentecost, was an autonomous organization.

By the very nature of the beginning, all the churches saw themselves as being part of the one universal church, without any formal overall organization. Now one had to be careful with whom one would associate oneself, since there were many false teachings coming up and roaming around in the Roman Empire.

This gave rise to the "Apostolic Fathers," like Polycarp (A.D. 69–156), bishop of Smyrna; Ignatius (A.D. 67–110), bishop of Antioch; and Papias (A.D. 70–155), bishop of Hierapolis. These were all disciples of the Apostle John, and all three suffered martyrdom at the hands of the Roman authorities.

The orthodox churches of the Roman Empire saw themselves as a unit and they held councils together to affirm their faith and share experiences and visions for the Church's future. Justin Martyr lived at this time, in whose days there were no reachable regions where Christ had not yet been preached. These were followed by Irenaeus (A.D.130–200). In his time, the churches issued the Apostles' Creed, which is still today the compact doctrinal basis of true Christian churches. It reads:

> "I believe in God the Father Almighty, Maker of heaven and earth,
> And in Jesus Christ his only begotten Son, our Lord,
> Who was conceived by the Holy Ghost,
> Born of the Virgin Mary,
> Suffered under Pontius Pilatus,
> Was crucified, dead, and buried:
> He descended into hell;
> The third day he rose again from the dead;
> He ascended into heaven,
> And sits on the right hand of God the Father Almighty;
> From thence he shall come to judge the quick and the dead.
> I believe in the Holy Ghost;
> The holy [General] Church;
> The Communion of Saints,
> The Forgiveness of sins,
> The Resurrection of the body,
> And the Life everlasting. Amen."

This all came about because of the opponents of the Christian faith and false Christian teachers. Nothing has been said against our faith throughout history until today that has not already been said by the infidels of those early years of the rise of the Christian Church.

Since that time, Christendom has been plagued by false teachings cropping up here and there. This is still happening today. It has the effect of confusing the general public regarding what is the true Christian faith, for some claim to be "the only true church," rejecting other Christian Churches altogether. This is a dangerous heresy. The fact is that there does not exist one church that is one hundred percent perfect in doctrine and conduct. Claiming that "ours is the only true one" is absolutely incorrect, both historically and doctrinally.

The churches that closest represent the true Christian faith are those called "Evangelical"—meaning "in tune with the Gospel"—and the "Fundamentalist" churches, who believe in the fundamental Christian teachings as represented in the Apostles' Creed. They are "orthodox," in the biblical sense, like Baptists, Methodists, Pentecostals, and other church groups that accept the Apostles' Creed and count themselves as being "Evangelical."

35.

THE RISE OF THE ROMAN CATHOLIC CHURCH

Catholics claim that the Apostle Peter was the first "Pope" (from the word *papa*, meaning "Father") of the Christian Church. In Matthew 23:9, Jesus forbids anyone from calling himself "father" of the church. Only one is supposed to be our father, and that is God in heaven. And yet, the developing stages of the Christian Church are:

1. Jesus Christ, founder, (27–31 A.D.)
2. The Apostles (31–90 A.D.)
3. The Apostolic Fathers (90–156 A.D.)
4. The Church Fathers (156–430 A.D)
5. The Patriarchs (430–590 A.D)
6. The Popes (590–present).
7. The Protestants and Evangelicals.

The most learned of the Church Fathers was Jerome (340–420 A.D). He translated the Bible into the Latin language. The book is called the "Vulgate," and it has been the basis for almost all the translations that came later. The most important theologian of the Church was Augustine, the

The Redemption Story

bishop of Hippo (354–430 A.D.). He moulded the doctrines of the Church systematically.

The reason these men are important is that, in the turmoil of their age, with all its conflicts and contradictions, they sought to stabilize the Christian Church and its teachings according to the words of the New Testament. They collected, evaluated, and selected the right Scriptures of the Old and New Testament under the guidance of the Holy Spirit, common sense, and historical truth.

The finished product is called the "Canon" (a "general rule or standard... officially recognized as genuine"[14]). Until 1456 A.D., when the German Johann Gutenberg invented the printing press, making the Bible cheaper to buy, the general laity was dependent upon the learned clergy to tell them what to believe.

This sad situation of the laity was abused by a number of Christian bishops who began to mix the Christian faith with heathen attitudes and rituals. As a result, the Christian Church became a ritualistic religion. Christ's and the Apostles' teachings were not practiced as recorded in the New Testament Scriptures. Teachings were adjusted at the pleasure of the clergy, and a power struggle among the bishops (some of which where called Popes) took place until the bishop of Rome finally emerged as the victorious top Pope. This happened around 600 A.D. The first real top Church leader called "Pope" was Gregory I (590–604 A.D.) Protestants and Evangelicals consider this date to be the beginning of the Roman Catholic Church proper.

---

[14] *Collins English Dictionary*. Glasgow, Scotland: Harper Collins (1995), p. 236.

Under Pope Stephen II (752–757 A.D.), the Frankish king Pepin conquered land in central Italy and gave it to the Pope of Rome. From this day forward, the Popes of Rome were not only leaders of a religion, but also earthly princes. Not satisfied with being the sovereign of a principality, the Roman Popes soon (after 858 A.D.) claimed authority over all the world's rulers as the top representative of Jesus Christ on earth. They assumed the title "Vicarius Filii Dei" (Representative of the Son of God) and "Pontifex Maximus" (the Highest Priest). The Roman Catholic Popes actually still claim to be this today. In return for this recognition, the Pope of Rome crowned the Frankish King Charlemagne with the title of a Roman Emperor ("Caesar," which became Germanized to "Kaiser"). The Pope and Emperor both renamed his realm "The Holy Roman Empire of the German Nation," a title the German Emperor had to surrender to Napoleon I of France in 1806. About 869 A.D., the Christian State Church split because of the demands and opposition of the bishops of Constantinople (now called Istanbul, in Turkey). The result was the independence of the Greek Orthodox Church of eastern Europe.

Because of the crimes being committed in both high and low places among the Roman Catholic clergy, many people grew unhappy with this Church. The Dark Ages of the Church had begun. Estranged Christian groups began to emerge. The trend became so strong that the Roman Catholic Church authorities undertook persecutions of the estranged Christians, to the point that from about 800 A.D. to the beginning of the nineteenth century, sixty to eighty million free Christians were murdered by the Catholic

Church. This certainly did not represent the teachings of Jesus Christ.

Because of the Church's progressing failures, the Protestant Reformation began in earnest in 1517 A.D. under such leaders as the German Martin Luther and the Swiss men John Calvin and Huldreich Zwingli. Free Evangelical churches came into existence, such as the Baptists and Mennonites. The Roman Church succeeded in totally killing all the Baptists in Germany and a lot of Mennonites until the latter moved away from Roman Catholic areas into the northern European kingdoms. These kingdoms had totally endorsed the Protestant position, not only for religious reasons, but also political ones. This religious schism in Europe led to the Thirty Years War, which together with the Black Death epidemic reduced the German population from twenty-five million to five million people. The Peace of Westphalia in 1648 ended with the Protestants keeping their freedom, but the Evangelicals still had many struggles to endure before they also were granted freedom of religion.

36.

THE EVANGELICAL REVIVALS (1170 A.D.— PRESENT)

The word "Evangelical" also encompasses the meaning, "in likeness of the life and teachings of Jesus Christ." It is a transliteration from the Greek word *Evaggelion*, which means "the Good News." Eventually, it became anglicized to "Gospel." The word "revival," in the Evangelical sense, means "a return to the original Christian faith and lifestyle as preached by Christ and the Apostles." So the Evangelical revivals were in fact a restoration of the faith and life of the original Church founded by Jesus Christ Himself.

The beginning of this movement goes back to the Waldensians of the twelfth century, whose name comes from a rich and learned merchant of the city of Lyons, France by the name of Pierre Waldo, who translated the Vulgate into the Provencial language, preached the true Gospel, and was banished for that by the Roman Pope. His movement spread throughout Europe from France to Hungary and the Alps to the Baltic Sea. The Roman Church succeeded in destroying them, except for a few right under the Pope's nose in the city of Rome and a few more in the secret

The Redemption Story

places within the mountains of the Alps. The later Waldensians accepted the theology of the Swiss reformers.

John Huss, Rector of the University of Prague, who was tortured to death at the Roman Catholic Church council of Constance (1414–1418), had a lot of followers in Bohemia of Czechoslovakia. They called themselves, in Latin, "Unitas Fratrum," which means "United Brotherhood," and despite of the Roman Catholic persecutions, they continued to prosper until many of them emigrated to the Protestant kingdom of Saxony, in modern day Germany, around 1725 A.D. There, this movement was rejuvenated under the guardianship of Count Nikolaus Ludwig Zinzendorf (1700–1760). Zinzendorf gave them a refuge on his estate, called Herrnhut. On August 27, 1727, the Holy Spirit fell on the whole assembly of three hundred brethren, similar to what happened on first Christian Pentecost in 31 A.D. As a result of this experience, the Unitas Fratrum began to send out missionaries as far as Greenland. They were the first Evangelical overseas missionaries in history. They are also known to us as the Moravian Church, or Fellowship of the Brethren, which still exists today. They didn't see themselves as a narrow minded church organization, but rather gladly friends of the many Evangelical groups that arose.

Through Zinzendorf himself, the original Gospel was proclaimed in Pennsylvania, where he established a number of Unitas Fratrum assemblies. Zinzendorf ordained Peter Boehler, who strongly influenced the Anglican clergyman John Wesley. Wesley became a turf-breaking evangelist, speaking in churches and out in the open. At that time, the camp meetings began, especially in the United States. Great revivals ensued in which many people not only accepted the Lord Jesus as their Saviour and Lord, but also were baptized in the Holy Spirit. At first, they did not understand what had happened to them, except that they noticed a fresh zeal and "fire" to win others for the Lord Jesus Christ. This caused the formation of the Methodist Church, followed by the Holiness Church, both of which named the baptism in the Holy Spirit "the Second Blessing." The final step of the growth of the Evangelical movement to this day is the rise of the Pentecostal and Charismatic Movements.

37.

A Short History of the Pentecostal/ Charismatic Revivals

According to most encyclopedias, the Pentecostal movement began in the Azusa Street Chapel in Los Angeles in 1907. However, my personal studies uncover a different story.

"[In 300 A.D.] dry formal orthodox men began even then to ridicule whatever gifts they had not themselves; and to decry them all, as either madness or imposture," writes

John Wesley.[15] About 400 A.D. the Church began to substitute the baptism in the Holy Spirit, including the gift of speaking in an unknown language, with the celebration of communion. They imposed the Latin language upon all their churches to replace speaking in other tongues. The Protestants inherited that trend and changed the name of "communion" to "confirmation."

Emperor Charlemagne believed that Christian believers could enjoy the gifts of the Holy Spirit. Under the Waldensians, many experienced the baptism in the Holy Spirit and spoke in other tongues. The first speaking in an unknown and unlearned language is a supernatural outward physical sign that an individual has indeed been baptized in the Holy Spirit. Historical evidences in the New Testament agree to this.

Around 1600, baptism in the Holy Spirit began to happen among the "Covenanters." In 1685, this also happened among the "Huguenots" of France. In 1710, many were baptized in the Holy Spirit among the French "Camisards." Even young boys preached mighty sermons under the anointing of the Holy Spirit. Then there was the Moravian Pentecost. In the Northampton Revival in Massachusetts in 1735, people were baptized in the Holy Spirit with all its accompanying physical effects. The same happened in the Scottish-Irish Revival in Kentucky in 1800.

Further reports of the experience of baptism in the Holy Spirit come from Edward Irving (1828), Miss Mary Campbell (1830), George and James MacDonald (1840), and Mrs.

---

[15] Kingston, Charles J.E. *Fullness of Power*. London, UK: Elim Publishing House (1965).

Michael Baxter (1885). The German Baptist preacher Dr. F.B. Meyer reports the same experiences among the Baptists of Estonia in 1895. In 1896, during a Holiness Church meeting in Cherokee County, North Carolina, the Holy Spirit came down and baptized a number of worshippers. In Kazakhstan in about 1750, the Holy Spirit baptized many Christians who were estranged from the Russian Orthodox Church. Since they didn't have the guidance of an educated pastor, many of them became entangled in Asian cultic beliefs. However, the true Evangelicals among them sent missionaries to Armenia. Many Armenians were baptized in the Holy Spirit; so many, in fact, that the Armenian Catholic Church felt threatened and began to persecute the Pentecostal believers. This caused many of them to emigrate to the United States, where they settled in southern California. While there, they lost the typical Pentecostal zeal to preach the Gospel to others.

When the Azusa Street revival broke out in 1907, they were astonished that God also sent down His Holy Spirit on non-Armenians. At the beginning of the twentieth century, it pleased God to pour out His Holy Spirit in places all around the world—in the United States, Germany, Wales, Norway, Sweden, Denmark, England, Finland, France, Holland, Austria, Poland and the Baltic states, India, China, Hong Kong, Africa, Chile, and Brazil. This movement caused a lot of contradiction and confusion among those who had no idea what the real Pentecost was all about. They banished the Pentecostal believers from their original home churches and thus forced the excommunicated Christians to band together in ever growing groups. In Canada, the largest Pentecostal group is the fellowship of the Pentecostal Assemblies of Canada.

The Pentecostal movement is now accepted as an Evangelical church. It has become the largest Evangelical movement in the world, being superseded only by the Roman Catholic Church in membership. There is even the prospect that the Catholic Church will become second in size to the Pentecostal churches in the next twenty years.

In the Pentecostal Movement, God has restored the powerful works that were being performed in the first century apostolic Church to produce converts, healings, baptisms in the Holy Spirit, miracles, and even occasionally the raising of the dead. It is said that the powerful move of God through the Pentecostal Movement is greater than the mission work of Paul. This is a first in church history. The fastest growth of this movement takes place today in Asia, Africa, and South America.

Since 1960, God has begun to send another wave of Pentecostalism in many other Church denominations, and these churches no longer excommunicate new Pentecostal believers, but rather tolerate them within their own ranks. This movement is called the Charismatic Movement. It appears that the Pentecostal and Charismatic movements bring many believers of many different churches together in a spirit of understanding and love. We see this as a sign that the promised return of the Lord Jesus Christ is indeed near at hand.

38.

SIGNS THAT THE RETURN OF OUR LORD JESUS IS NEAR AT HAND

While it is impossible to provide an exhaustive list of signs that the Second Coming is soon in coming, here are the most relevant indications:

1. The most important sign is the resurrection of the state of Israel. The prophets Isaiah, Ezekiel, Daniel, and Zechariah speak of the reestablishment of the state of Israel in Palestine. Three returns to the land by the Jews are mentioned. The first return was from Assyria, the second return was from Babylonia, and finally a last return when the returnees would "fly" back home to the land of Israel, which is only possible in our modern times (Isaiah 11:12–14, 60:8–9). The Jews shall come home both with ships and airplanes from the distant lands. The modern return of the Jews to their ancient homeland began in the late 1800s. It was also foretold by some Evangelical pastors, who were well-acquainted with the Old Testament prophecies.

However, there has always been a Jewish minority living in Israel throughout the centuries, even though they were suppressed and suffered much by various political and

The Redemption Story

religious powers. Their continuous existence in that land confirms to the Jews the right to claim that territory as their original homeland, a thing which the Moslem fanatics deny. This is why there is a constant conflict going on between Israel and the Moslems.

Until the mass immigration of Jews back home, they were too few to reestablish a Jewish national authority in Palestine. That finally happened on May 14, 1948, when with a population of 720,000, the modern state of Israel was proclaimed.

Jesus Himself taught that the generation that lives at the return of old Jerusalem to Jewish authority shall experience all remaining events from that point in time until His personal return to Israel (Luke 21:24).

All of Jerusalem returned under Jewish authority in June 1967. The longest lifespan of one generation, as ordained by God, is 120 years (Genesis 6:3). Moses thought that the expected lifespan of a person was seventy to eighty years (Psalm 90:10). However, he himself made it to an age of 120 years. If his thinking is correct, then Jesus should return no later than 2047. If it goes according to God's statement in Genesis, then His return could be delayed up to 2087. However, it will probably happen a lot sooner.

The return of Jesus Christ will be preceded by a certain solar eclipse, which will darken the "seat of the beast" shortly before His appearance. Such eclipses will occur in the years 2053, 2059, 2072, 2075, 2081, and 2082. In conjunction with a solar eclipse, there is to be a meteorite shower of a great magnitude.

But what is the "seat of the beast," you ask? In Daniel 2, there is a description of a great statue with a golden head and ten toes. This statue is intended to be viewed as a metaphor of human history.

According to the view of many Evangelicals, the golden head stands for Babylon (Daniel 2:38), the chest stands for Medo-Persia (Daniel 2:39), the lower body stands for the Macedonian Empire (Daniel 2:39), and the two legs stand for the Roman Empire. The one leg represents the Latin (Western) part and the other leg the Greek (Eastern) part of the Roman Empire. Next, we have the toes—ten of them, each corresponding to a modern nation. Five of these spring from the Latin Roman Empire, and the other five spring from the Greek Roman Empire. I found that there are only five Latin nations that could be said to be direct children of Rome: Italy, Austria, France, Spain, and Britain. The rest could be considered grandchildren at best (for instance, Portugal, breaking away from Spain). On the Greek side, there are also only five possibilities: Greece, Bulgaria, Romania, Albania, and the former Yugoslavia. There are no others.

Next, I began searching for the "little horn" of Daniel 7. A "little horn" could be said to be a "mini-nation." I found that on the Latin side there are seven such mini-nations—and on the Greek side, none. After researching the origins of the seven Latin mini-nations, I came to realize that only one of them truly matches the prophecy (Daniel 7:8,20–24). This mini-nation must have grown out of the ten nations, but also be distinct politically. The only possible mini-nation that fits the bill is San Marino, a tiny country landlocked near the Adriatic coast of Italy.

The Redemption Story

San Marino is very old—the oldest continuous republic in the world, having been founded in 301 A.D. This means that it existed during the final 175 years of the Latin Roman Empire. It is governed completely differently from any other nation, controlled by two *capitani reggenti* (captains regent). Located about 280 kilometres north of Rome, it is perched on a mountain named Monte Titano, or "Mountain of the Giant." On this mountain, there are three castles named Guaita (a feminine word meaning "whining"), Cesta ("a large basket"), and Montale ("moan," "groan," "lament"). My hair just about stood on end when I discovered the meaning of the name of two of the castles sitting on this mountain—the castle Torre Guaita, which could be referred to as "The Tower of the Lamenting Woman," and the Torre Montale, which could be referred to as "The Tower of Lamentation." This appears to hint at the sufferings of the Bride of Christ (Christians) during the Great Tribulation period. In addition to this observation, it must be noted that the borders of San Marino show the outline of a human face looking east. Indeed, the San Marino coat of arms shows three castles on a mountain. It seems likely that Antichrist will use this mini-nation as his pedestal to break into world politics.

2. The gospel of the kingdom of Jesus Christ will be preached throughout the whole world. Though not all languages have a translation of the New Testament as yet, the Christian message is reaching out to whoever has a radio or TV around the entire globe, if they care to listen.

3. There will be "distress of the nations with perplexity" (Luke 21:25). This is what we are going through right now with the current global economic crisis. A final crisis will emerge just before Christ's return, according to Revelation 18.

4. Israel will increasingly have a hard time politically and militarily, until they have nothing more left of their land than half the city of Jerusalem, according to Zechariah 14.

5. Sea and land storms will increase in severity, caused as we experience it by ongoing climate change.

6. A man called Antichrist by the Bible will gain control of many countries in Europe on old Roman territory. Daniel 2 speaks of ten nations. That should not be taken to mean that there will not be more nations included in that confederacy, however. The basis for this to happen already exists in the European Union, with their common Euro currency and gradual efforts to create a United States of Europe. Antichrist will also meddle in Middle East conflicts and create a short-lived peace between Israel and its enemies. He will be accepted by the Jews as their Messiah.

To achieve this, he must be at least half Jewish and prove his descendancy from the family of David, otherwise the Jews would never accept him. He will make a seven-year treaty with Israel. Under his protection, the new Jewish temple will be built in Jerusalem. Already in existence now is a Jewish group called the "Temple Institute," who have already created all the temple instruments and have plans for the building of the third temple.

After three and a half years, Antichrist will show his true face and place an image of himself in this temple. This image will be able to speak with a human voice, which obviously is possible today in the form of a computer. This blas-

The Redemption Story 123

phemy will bring the Jews into a rage. Antichrist will break the treaty and fight the Jewish nation, and also the Evangelical Christians, because of their support of Israel.

So who is this man, really? His name is given in Revelation 13:18, in the number 666. These numbers stand for letters in the Hebrew language, and they spell "Terasu," a name that with variants is relatively common among Jews and Arabs. "According to a number of ancient Christians, Antichrist will be born of a demon-possessed woman impregnated by Satan."[16] Indications from scripture are that he will have six fingers per hand and six toes per foot. This is also hinted at by the shape of Greece (the dragon's right forearm). Please see the map of Europe in the next chapter. According to Daniel 11:37-38, he will *"regard neither the God of his fathers nor the desire of women."* He will be able to perform miracles. He will be assassinated by Jewish rebels and experience a resurrection. His right eye will be totally blinded, and one arm will be crippled (Zechariah 11:17).

A number of Bible teachers believe that this person will come to rule the whole earth. While Revelation 13 appears to indicate this, the Book of Daniel does not foresee such a thing. Since there cannot be a contradiction in Bible teaching, we must look for a sensible solution to the discrepancy. The problem lies in understanding the little word "all" in the text. It does not mean "everything without exclusion," but is rather a generalization, just as people now use it commonly. The Greek term for this phenomenon is "Synecdoche," which is a figure of speech that means "that

---

[16] Gassner, Johann Joseph. *Nützlicher Unterricht wider den Teufel zu Streiten.* Warngau: Die Fundgrube (1952), paraphrased.

what one observes," and not "that which is the entirety of reality."

This becomes evident when you consider that many nations of our globe fight Antichrist and his armies at Armageddon in Israel. This happens at the end of the Great Tribulation, with an army of more than two hundred million soldiers. Some participating nations are mentioned in the Prophet Ezekiel 38:13—Sheba, Dedan (Arabian states), Tarshish (Spain and other nations related to Spain), and the "young lions thereof," which points to relatively young nations descending from the Tarshish nations, most likely the Americas. Then there are Rosh, Mesach, and Tubal (Russia). In Revelations 16:12–14, the kings of the East and the "whole world" are mentioned. Obviously they will not be subject to Antichrist, seeing as they are his enemies.

A further hint of the "Free World" existing beside Antichrist's dominion is found in Ezekiel 39:6, which speaks of people living in "security in the coastlands" on the day Jesus Christ destroys the world with fire. These "coastlands" are obviously living outside of the hemisphere of Antichrist. These are the ones who live as in "Noah's days," carelessly going about their business as they have always done until the Son of Man is revealed (Luke 17:26–30). Christ's return will come to them as an unexpected shock.

The Lord Jesus says that Israel's three and a half year tribulation period will be shortened, or else all mankind would be destroyed (Matthew 24:22). He probably has nuclear weapons in mind. The figures given in Daniel say that the Great Tribulation will last three and a half years—*"a time, and times, and half a time"* (Revelation 12:14). Daniel, in Daniel 12:11, is specific and says that it will last 1,290 days. In Daniel 8, he states that the actual tribulation will last 2,300 mornings and evenings (meant as sacrifices). That is two sacrifices per day, resulting in 1,150 days, showing a shortening of the tribulation by 140 days. This shortening is brought about by the appearance of Jesus Christ with His saved people and angels. This happens at the most critical point in Israel's history, according to Revelation 19 and Zechariah 14.

It is said that no one can know the exact day of this event. This is not quite correct, either. True, today no one can know the exact day the Lord Jesus will return. However, the people who live on the day the treaty between Israel and Antichrist is signed can know that the coming of the Lord is exactly 2410 days ahead. The reason is probably to comfort the persecuted sufferers of that time. However, the Bible even gives us the time of the day that the Lord Jesus will return to Jerusalem and Israel. In Zechariah 14:7, it says, *"at evening time it shall happen."* That means Jerusalem time.

39.

THE CONFLICT OF THE "GREAT TRIBULATION" IS IMPRINTED IN THE GEOGRAPHICAL SHAPES OF EUROPE

Of all continents of the Earth, Europe has the most geographical shapes that are similar to animal forms or peculiarities that are easily recognizable. There are ten such images. These images in Europe represent a pictorial story of the conflict of the Great Tribulation between Antichrist and his empire against Israel. It is a lot easier to discern these images on the face of the earth than it is to imagine the images of the star pictures of the Zodiac, for example, which have been historically accepted for millennia.

1. Everybody knows about the territorial shape that reminds us of a boot. It is the nation of Italy. It is the first obvious image, a reference to the boot that military men used to wear. It is positioned on the map in a kicking position, as if the boot is kicking the island of Sicily, which one can view as a rock. It represents the Kingdom of God which will crush the domain of Antichrist (the boot) and replace it according to Daniel 2:39, 44–45.

2. The rock (Sicily) also stands for Jesus Christ, who is called a "rock" in Isaiah 8:13–14 and Romans 9:32–33.

3. In the north, you have the Scandinavian Peninsula (Norway and Sweden), looking like a lion. The Scandinavians know this and call their country "The Lion of the North." It represents the Lion of Judah, the Lord Jesus Christ.

4. Next you will find the Danish peninsula of Jutland. The Danes look at it as the head and face of a small man. It represents Antichrist, also called "the little Horn" that spoke (Daniel 7:8).

5. Moving west, there is the island of Great Britain. The part of it that is called England looks like a woman's head and face. The woman's mouth is the Thames River, flowing into the English Channel. The British speak of it as a "mouth."

6. Her body is France, and she points toward Jutland, the Antichrist, with her arm and hand represented by Belgium and the Netherlands. This woman, called "the Great Harlot" (Revelation 19:2), is the theme of Revelation 17 and 18. It is a religious power headquartered in Rome, probably the Roman Catholic Church. That church has drifted away from the simple Christian faith to become a ritualistic religious empire. It also has the blood of the free Christian martyrs on its hands. According to this prophecy, it might just be the power which eventually supports Antichrist against Israel.

7. The border of France along Germany and Switzerland has the shape of a half chalice. When folded over symmetrically, you see a complete chalice. It is a representation of the "golden cup" in the hand of Babylon the Great sitting on the Great Dragon, who represents the antichristian empire.

8. The head of this Great Dragon we find in the image of the Black Sea. It looks like the head of a reptile, with something like a horn shape on its head (Daniel 7:7 and 19–27; Revelation 12: 3–9 and 13:1–10). It is viewed from the right side, and there is no geological item that could represent an eye. This agrees with the statement from the prophet Zechariah: *"His right eye shall be totally blinded"* (Zechariah 11:17).

9. In the nation of Greece, the regions called "Achaia" (or Hellas) and "Peloponnesus" look like a lizard's arm with six toes.

10. The area south of the city Thessalonica, called "Khalkidhiki," looks like a crippled arm with only three fingers. It corresponds with the words, *"His arm shall completely wither"* (Zechariah 11:17). These images are positioned accordingly with the Dragon's head, the Black Sea.

The overarching story these images tell is this: "Jesus Christ as the Lion of Judah comes from the North upon Antichrist, Babylon the Great, and Antichrist's empire, called the 'Fiery Red Dragon' (Revelation 12:1), who is moving against the little land of Israel." Who created this phenomenon on the face of the Earth? Obviously not the Theory of Evolution, but the Designer: Almighty God. This phenomenon is actually a proof of God's existence, for the details are too numerous to allow for chance.

The Redemption Story

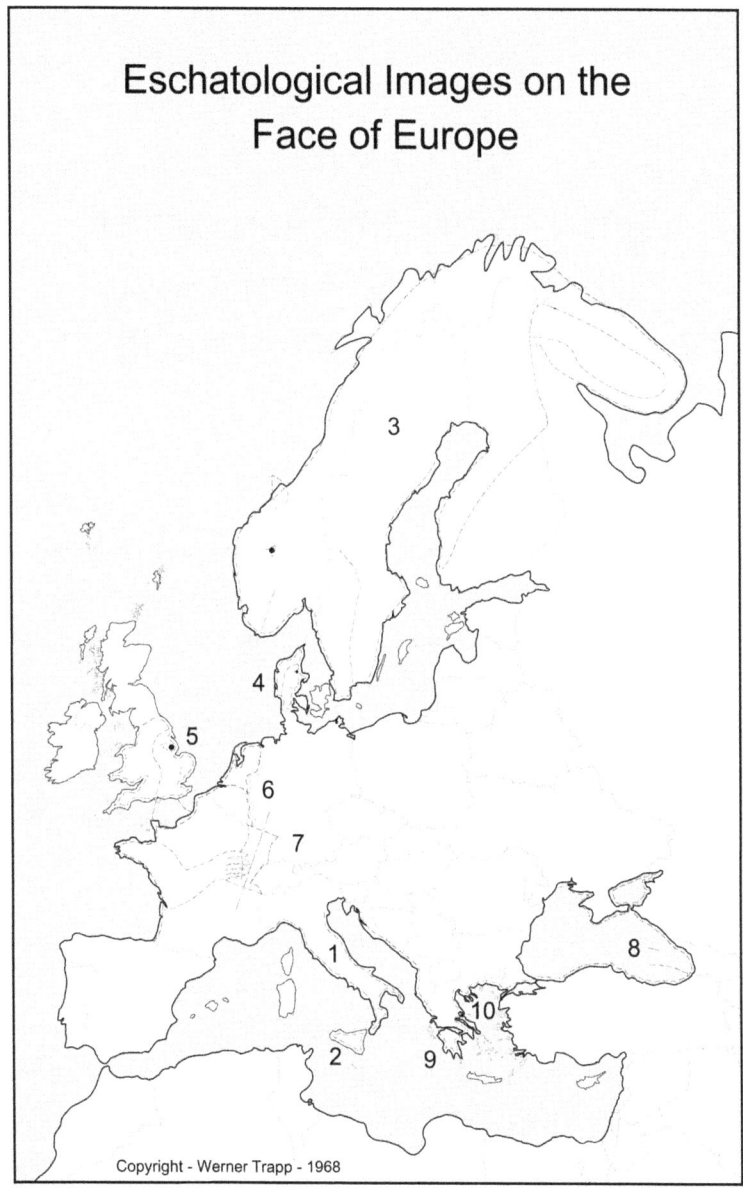

40.

WHAT WILL HAPPEN AFTER THE DEFEAT OF ANTI-CHRIST AND SATAN AT ARMAGEDDON?

After the "kings of the East" (Russia, China, and India) have defeated Antichrist, they will continue the battle against Israel. They will fight their way against Jewish resistance to Jerusalem. God Himself will do things to them like throw giant hailstones upon them (Revelation 16:21). Once the enemy has entered Jerusalem and the Jews are at the end of their desperate resistance, Jesus Christ will come from heaven, with angels and saved people following Him, and bring the battle to a victorious end. At the same time, the rapture will take place.

What is the rapture? It is the removal of Christian believers from this earth and their meeting with Jesus Christ in the air at His return. Most Evangelicals believe that these people will be raptured before the Great Tribulation begins. These people are called "Pretribs." Some believe that this event will happen in the middle of Antichrist's seven-year rule. They are called "Midtribs." Others believe that this shall happen after the end of the Great Tribulation. They are called "Posttribs." Who is right?

For me, it is somewhat perplexing that people are so confused about this subject, since it is actually relatively easy to determine the right answer. First, let me quote the Lord Jesus, for He should certainly know the truth. He states plain and simple, *"Immediately after the tribulation of those days... He will send His angels with a great sound of a trumpet, and they will gather together His elect [Jewish and Gentile Christians] from the four winds [North, South, East and West], from one end of heaven [the air] to the other"* (Matthew 24:29,31). So this meeting will be "after" the tribulation and in the air. That is clearly the rapture.

In Luke 17:34–35, we find the word "taken" in connection with Christ's visible revelation to the world. Some scholars believe that the meaning of the word "taken" means "taken in judgment," while those who are left will survive for the millennium. A close study of this word reveals that the opposite is true. The word "taken"—in Greek, *paralambanetai*—also means "received," so the elect will be received into the air heaven to join Christ. Examples are the story of Enoch: *"Enoch walked with God; and he was not (anymore on earth, my comment), for God took him"* (Genesis 5:24, emphasis mine). Where did God take him? In judgment? Certainly not. He took Enoch to Himself in heaven as a reward for walking with God.

In 2 Kings, it says about the prophet Elijah: *"It came to pass, when the Lord was about to take up Elijah into heaven..."* (2 Kings 2:1, emphasis mine). The context of the word "take" in these passages indicates a removal from earth to heaven. Such is also the meaning in Luke. (Other passages exist in Ezekiel 3:12, 11:24, and 43:5; Isaiah 53:8; and Acts 1:2,9,11,22; 8:33).

Actually, the rapture is a mystery. To solve this mystery, note the unity of these three references. You will find that they share a common thread:

1. In Revelation 10:7, it says about this mystery: *"In the days of the <u>sounding of the seventh angel</u> [the last trumpet], when he is about to sound, the mystery of God would be finished, as He declared to His servants the prophets"* (emphasis mine).

2. Go to 1 Corinthians 15:51–52: *"Behold, I tell you a mystery: We shall not all sleep, but we shall all be changed—in a moment, in the twinkling of an eye, <u>at the last trumpet</u>. For the trumpet will sound, and the dead will be raised incorruptible, and we shall be changed"* (emphasis mine).

3. Go to 1 Thessalonians 4:15–17. There, Paul writes, *"This we say to you by the word of the Lord, that we who are alive and remain until the coming of the Lord will <u>by no means precede</u> those who are asleep [dead]. For the Lord Himself will descend from heaven with a shout, with the voice of an archangel, and with the trumpet of God. And the dead in Christ <u>will rise first</u>. Then we who are alive and remain [through the Great Tribulation] shall be caught up together with them in the clouds to meet the Lord in the air. And thus we shall always be with the Lord"* (emphasis mine). Here, the Apostle combines the first resurrection with the rapture. Since the first resurrection appears to take place *after* the Great Tribulation, the rapture is bound to happen at the same time. The prophet Zechariah speaks very clearly about this event: *"Behold, the day of the Lord is coming... I will gather all the nations to battle against Jerusalem; the city shall be taken, the houses plundered, and the women rav-*

ished. *Half of the city shall go into captivity, but the remnant of the people shall not be cut off from the city. Then the Lord will go forth and fight against those nations, as He fights in the day of battle. And in that day His feet will stand on the mount of Olives, which faces Jerusalem on the east [landing there, coming from heaven]. And the Mount of Olives shall be split in two, from east to west… Then you shall flee through My mountain valley… Thus the Lord my God will come, and all the saints with [Him]"* (Zechariah 14:1–5).

The "saints" are God's trusting people from the Old Testament, as well as the Christians of the New Testament—that is us! Considering this last quotation, it is my opinion that the rapture comes before the final blow to the godless world that is recorded in Ezekiel 38 and 39.

41.
THINGS THAT HAPPEN AFTER THE RAPTURE

Revelation 19 gives us the story of Christ's coming and discusses its after effects. Ezekiel 38 and 39 also deal with this issue in great detail, making it clear why a rapture of God's children away from this earth will become necessary. God says, *"I will send fire on Magog and on those who live in security in the coastlands. Then they shall know that I am the Lord"*

(Ezekiel 39:6). Also see Isaiah 66:15. "Magog" is the northern confederation (Russia) that together with the "kings of the East" fight against Antichrist. After they have defeated him, they will move against Israel to create "order" in the Middle East. The Israelis will resist them all the way until half of Jerusalem is taken (Zechariah 14). The "coastlands" are the rest of the world, which in the eyes of the ancients could be reached only by ship. This land also includes the Americas. The rapture is necessary, therefore, to get God's people out of the way of this fire that will destroy all people living in the world. These are people who have not obeyed God's call to honour His Son Jesus Christ by accepting Him as their Saviour and Lord.

There is one exception. Jesus says, *"Let the little children come to Me, and do not forbid them; for of such is the kingdom of God"* (Luke 18:16). He is talking about children thirteen years old and younger. From that age forward, they are called "Bar Mitzvah" (Sons of the Commandment), held to be mature enough for personal responsibility. So these kids will not perish along with the rest of mankind. How will they be saved? This is a secret only God knows. Perhaps they too will join in the rapture. However, they will be around on earth to continue their earthly lives.

Now you have nations of children all around the world. Who governs them and takes care of them? God speaks through Isaiah and says, *"It shall be that I will gather all nations and tongues; and they shall come and see My glory [see God's person]. I will set a sign among them; and those among them [of Israel] who escape I will send to the nations: to Tarshish and Pul and Lud, who draw the bow, and Tubal and Javan, to the coast-*

The Redemption Story

lands afar off who have not heard My fame nor seen My glory. And they [the Israeli military] shall declare My glory among the Gentiles… [and] all flesh shall come to worship before Me" (Isaiah 66:18–20,23).

See also Zechariah 14. In Revelation 20, it says that the Christian martyrs of the Great Tribulation period who were resurrected would sit on thrones and govern with Christ for a thousand years. Then there are all those millions of faithful people who have returned with Christ. They too shall be kings (governors) and priests with Christ. Remember, according to 1 Thessalonians 4:15–17, these people will now have spiritual bodies that cannot die, but are eternal.

This earthly kingdom of Christ is called "the Millennium." In it, there shall finally be peace on earth. In Isaiah 65, we learn that the long lifespans enjoyed by the people at the beginning of Bible history will be restored. Someone who is a hundred years old will be called "a child." God's literal presence will be with the people. Even among the animals, there will be peace so that even lions will eat vegetation. Nature will be restored to its virginity and all the people will enjoy the fruits thereof. What a wonderful time that will be, but this is not the end.

42.

WHAT WILL HAPPEN IN ISRAEL RIGHT AFTER THE RETURN OF THE LORD JESUS CHRIST?

Ezekiel 39–48 and Zechariah 14 prophecy about this period of time. At the same time of the Lord Jesus' return, there will be a fantastic earthquake in Israel. In the area of Beth-El (about twelve kilometres north of Jerusalem), there will be a high mountain. On it, the Millennial Temple shall stand. On the east side of this temple, a "river of living water" (Ezekiel 47) will begin. It will run through Jerusalem. Within the city limits, it will divide into two branches (Zechariah 14), dividing the city into three parts. One branch will run into the Mediterranean Sea, and the other down into the Dead Sea. It will freshen most of its waters so that sea fish will prosper there. Only the end of the Dead Sea will remain salty. On the banks of this river, special trees will grow that sound like they could be similar to the Tree of Life in Revelation 22. They will bear fruit every month. Their fruit will be food and the leaves of these trees will be used for medicine.

In Daniel 12, we learn that every person who lives to see the 1235th day after Antichrist sets up his image in the

The Redemption Story

Jewish temple at Jerusalem will be "blessed." Why? It will be the day that the Lord Jesus Christ is crowned King of the whole world. He will keep the Passover Feast, which He has promised He will do when the Kingdom of God, through His return, comes to dominate the whole earth (Luke 22:16). So it appears that Christ comes back during the winter, and He will be crowned King of the world in the spring at Passover. There will also be an earthly partner of His person in the form of the Jewish governor who led Israel through the tribulation period. This governor and the high priest officiating in the rebuilt temple of Jerusalem are called the "two olive trees" and the "two anointed ones" (Zechariah 4, Revelation 11:3–4). The governor and his sons (Ezekiel 46:16) will represent Jesus Christ for the land of Israel. The territory of Israel will for the first time encompass everything God once promised to give them from the Brook of Egypt (Wadi El Arish) up to close to the city Tyre in Lebanon, and as far east as the Euphrates River in Syria. The land will be divided to the twelve tribes with the governor's portion in the middle of the land, near to the new temple at Beth-El. This is the place that Jacob in antiquity selected as being the House of God (Genesis 28:17–22). Finally, the time for it will have arrived.

In Ezekiel, we learn that the Jews will go out from their towns and burn the weapons of the enemy, and it will take them seven years to get rid of everything. The leader of the Magog confederation, "Gog," will be buried in Israel. For seven months, the Jews will gather the human remains of the enemy soldiers and the fallen of Israel and bury them.

All the nations of the world will send representatives annually to Jerusalem to worship God there. They will keep the Feast of Tabernacles together with the Jewish people (in September or October) and there will be threats for noncompliance (Zechariah 14:16–19). The temple animal sacrifices will be restored. For what purpose, I am not sure. My guess is that it will be a memorial, reflecting back to the sacrificial death of our Lord Jesus Christ similar to why we celebrate the Lord's supper (communion) in churches today. This must be so, since:

1. The sacrifice of animals cannot remove sin (Hebrews 10:4).
2. We have been sanctified (cleansed from sin) through the offering of the body of Jesus Christ once for all (Hebrews 10:10).

This thousand year reign of Christ on earth will also come to an end. Despite the fact that even the devil and his angels will be bound in hell during this period of time, the sin condition of some people will cause a rebellion against Him in spite of all the advantages and blessings they have enjoyed. The devil will be let loose from hell and be allowed to stir the rebels up to surround Jerusalem, but again, fire from God will destroy them. After this will follow the Last Judgment, according to God's plan.

43.

THE GREAT JUDGEMENT DAY AT THE GREAT WHITE THRONE

Though we talk about the "Great Judgment Day," this judgment will continue over a longer period of time than just one day, because the Bible in Revelation 20 does not confine it to a specific day. Many Evangelicals are convinced that everyone who has to stand for judgment at the Great White Throne will be automatically condemned to the eternal hell, called "the Lake of Fire" and "the second death." With closer examination of the context of these verses from the prophets Isaiah, Ezekiel, and Zechariah, it appears that there will be nations (ethnic people groups) on the new earth (Revelation 21:24 and Zechariah 14:16–19).

Since all Christians are to live with Christ in the new city of Jerusalem, there is no choice but to assume that the "nations" that bring their glory and honour into the New Jerusalem are the survivors of the Great White Throne judgment. Their names were found recorded in the twice mentioned Book of Life.

Who are these people? They are all the people still remaining in the world who didn't hear the Good News about the salvation given through Jesus Christ. They would have accepted Him, if they would have had the chance, according to the foreknowledge of God. The people who were condemned to eternal hell are those who were given that chance, but refused to accept our Lord Jesus Christ. So it is not God's fault if they find themselves in the eternal hell, but rather their own. God does not send anyone to hell, but rather *"desires that all [people] to be saved and to come to the knowledge of the truth"* (1 Timothy 2:4). Therefore He has given our Lord Jesus Christ to become the Saviour of ALL people (1 Timothy 4:10).

The Apostle John tells us, *"I saw a new heaven and a new earth, for the first heaven and the first earth had passed away"* (Revelation 21:1). According to Revelation 20:11, *"The [old] earth and the [old] heaven fled away. And there will be no place found for them,"* as they were shot into the unending outer space to disappear forever.

While there can still be tears in the present heaven (Revelation 5:4–5), in this new future heaven life will be totally different. *"Then I, John, saw the holy city, New Jerusalem, coming down out of heaven from God, prepared as a bride adorned for her husband. And I heard a loud voice from heaven saying, 'Behold, the tabernacle of God is with [people], and He will dwell with them, and they shall be His people. God Himself will be with them and be their God. And God will wipe away every tear from their eyes; there shall be no more death, nor sorrow, nor crying. There shall be no more pain, for the former things have passed away.' Then He who sat on the throne said, 'Behold, I make all things new.' And He said to me, 'Write, for these words are true and faithful.'"* (Revelation 21:2–5).

44.
WHERE IS HEAVEN NOW, AND WHAT CAN WE FIND IN IT?

The Scriptures actually reveal three heavens to us. That there are more than one is obvious in the very first statement in Genesis 1:1. The Hebrew word to look at is *shamayim*, which is a plural, translated as "heavens." As the Book of Genesis unfolds, we learn that the atmosphere around the earth is called "heaven." This is the first heaven. For example, the Bible says, *"By the word of the Lord the heavens were made"* (Psalm 33:6). At least two heavens are required to justify this plural statement. This is confirmed by King Solomon's words: *"Will God indeed dwell on the earth? Behold, heaven and the heaven of heavens cannot contain You"* (1 Kings 8:27). According to this, there are at least three heavens.

The second heaven is the heaven in which the stars and the planets exist.

The Apostle Paul tells of having visited the third heaven, which is God's abode (Deuteronomy 10:14). Paul says, *"I know a man in Christ who fourteen years ago—whether in the body I do not know, or whether out of the body I do not* know, God knows—such a one was caught up to the third heaven. And I know such a man—whether in the body or out of the body I do not know, God knows—how he was caught up into Paradise and heard inexpressible words, which it is not lawful for a [person] to utter. Of such a one I will boast"* (2 Corinthians 12:2–4).

As already noted in Chapter 1, the Bible speaks of God's abode *"on the farthest sides of the north"* (Isaiah 14:13). According to this statement, one of the stars or planets in this massive light is the third heaven, the abode of God.

The Book of Revelation gives us a number of evidences that the third heaven will be on a planet called the New Earth, for where God dwells, there heaven is. It has a capital city (Revelation 21:10). It contains metals, such as gold (Revelation 21:18) It contains precious stones and pearls (Revelation 21:19–21). It contains water, such as in the River of Life (Revelation 22:1). It contains plant life, such as the Tree of Life (Revelation 22:2–3), which brings fruit every month. The reference to monthly fruit even suggests that there will be a reckoning of time in heaven. This surely sounds different than the words in the old Gospel song, "When the trumpet of the Lord shall sound and time shall be no more…" Since plants need air and soil, heaven appears to be fully like a planet. God will move His heavenly atmosphere down to the new eternal earth (Revelation 21:1).

Right now, the heaven in the uttermost north is where the saved people of the earth go, those who accept Jesus as their personal Saviour and Lord and follow His teaching, after passing away. They will in future live in the New Jerusalem on that new earth while all others that made it through the Great White Throne judgment will be the nations that bring their glory to this capital city. I pray that all who read this book will be in that city one day.

What will life be like in that new heaven? Some people have really funny ideas about that. Some dream about floating on a cloud and playing a harp. Others figure we will eternally stand before the throne of God and worship Him. An atheist on a TV talk show once said that he would rather be eternally dead than eternally kneeling and worshipping God, as that would become awfully boring with time. Can't argue that one. So what will life really be like up there? While we must dig quite a bit in God's Word to find an answer, one thing is clear: We will never be bored.

It appears that there will be a lot of work to be done, one exciting project after another. There are a lot of planets in the cosmos for some grand projects. Besides this, the Lord Jesus once said: *"My Father has been working until now, and I have been working"* (John 5:17). In the Book of Revelation, we see the angels working. Another example of the Bible's attitude about work is found in Proverbs: *"The hand of the diligent will rule, but the lazy man will be put to forced labor… The lazy man does not roast what he took in hunting, but diligence is man's precious possession"* (Proverbs 12:24,27). These statements do suggest that in heaven there will also be work to be done.

Many of us will become rulers over a city or kings over a kingdom. Many of us will become priests. What does this mean? After all, in order to be a ruler or priest, you must have subjects of some kind. This brings me back to an earlier statement: All others that made it through the Great

White Throne judgment will be the nations that bring their glory to this capital of heaven, the New Jerusalem. It appears that these people will retain their physical nature, which is perishable. However, they will never perish, on account of the fruits and leaves of the Tree of Life, which grows there for this purpose.

We will also celebrate the biblical feasts in heaven (Zechariah 14:16). There will be rain (Zechariah 14:17). For what? For crops and for rivers and lakes, naturally. So there will be sunshine and clouds, too. There will be animals in heaven, like horses (Zechariah 14:21). In Revelation 4, living creatures are reported, such as lions, cattle, eagles, and sheep. In Romans 8, we are told of the resurrection of animals:

"For I consider that the sufferings of this present time are not worthy to be compared with the glory which shall be revealed in us. For the earnest expectation of the creation [the animal world] eagerly waits for the revealing of the sons [and daughters] of God. For the creation [the animal world] was subjected to futility, not willingly, but because of Him who subjected it in hope [of a resurrection]; because the creation [the creatures] itself also will be delivered from the bondage of corruption into the glorious liberty of the children of God. For we know that the whole creation [us and the animal world] groans and labors with birth pangs together until now. Not only that, but we also who have the firstfruits of the Spirit, even we ourselves groan within ourselves, eagerly waiting for the adoption, the redemption of our body [in the resurrection]" (Romans 8:18–27).

Jesus also said that there will be no more marriages, for we will be like the angels of God (Luke 20:34–38). Just

The Redemption Story

imagine what a wonderful life we will experience in heaven, with all that love and peace and happiness surrounding us eternally. No sin, no death, no sorrow, or any other negative thing around us anymore… just sheer delight and happiness. Best of all, we will see our Lord Jesus and our heavenly Father personally in all their heavenly glory. They will touch us and wipe away our tears. We will be one glorious family of God.

John says, in his first letter, *"Behold what manner of love the Father has bestowed on us, that we should be called children of God!… Beloved, now we are children of God; and it has not yet been revealed what we shall be, but we know that when He is revealed, we shall be like Him, for we shall see Him as He is. And everyone who has this hope in Him purifies himself, just as He is pure"* (1 John 3:1–3) In other words, John hints that we will be counted as gods, seeing as we will be part of God's family. Then there will not anymore be a Godhead of a Trinity, but a Godhead of Fourfulness: Father, Son, Holy Spirit, and the Church!

This was God's plan right from the beginning when he created Adam and Eve. Satan spoiled it for a time, but God recovered that position for us through our Lord Jesus Christ. Finally, full Redemption is completed. Amen!

BIBLIOGRAPHY

Collins English Dictionary. Glasgow, Scotland: Harper Collins (1995).

Dake, Finis Jennings. *Dake's Annotated Reference Bible*. Atlanta, GA: Dake Bible Sales (1963).

Grayzel, Solomon. *A History of the Jews*. Markham: Penguin (1984).

Grimberg, Carl. *Sveriges Historia För Folkskolan*. Stockholm: P.A. Norstedt & Sõners Förlag (1936).

Halley, Henry H. *Halley's Bible Handbook*. Grand Rapids, MI: Zondervan (1965).

Hauser, Rev. Cheryl. *Israel Teaching Letter*. Jerusalem: Bridges for Peace (2008).

Kingston, Charles J.E. *Fullness of Power*. London: Elim Publishing House (1965).

Lechler, Gotthard Viktor. *Johannes Hus*. Sweden: J.A. Lindblads Förlag (1915).

Matrisciana, C. & R. Oakland. *The Evolution Conspiracy*. Jacksonville Beach, FL: Jeremiah Films (1988).

May, Herbert G. *Oxford Bible Atlas*. London, UK: Oxford University Press (1970).

Navarra, Fernand. *Noah's Ark: I Touched It*. London, UK: Logos International (1974).

Nichol, John Thomas. *The Pentecostals*. Plainfield: Logos International (1945).

Nichols, Robert Hastings. *Growth of the Christian Church*. Philadelphia, PA: Westminster Press (1941).

Schäfer, Wilhelm. *Die Dreizehn Bücher der deutschen Seele*. München, Germany: Albert Langden/Georg Müller (1922).

Scofield, C.I. *The Scofield Reference Bible*. New York, NY: Oxford University Press (1945).

Spencer, Duane E. *The Gospel in the Stars*. San Antonio, TX: The Word of Grace (1972).

Stacke, Ludwig. *Römische Geschichte*. Oldenburg: Gerhard Stalling (1904).

Unger, Merrill F. *Ungers Bible Dictionary*. Chicago, IL: Moody Press (1965).

Whiston, William (translation). *Josephus*. Grand Rapids, MI: Kregel Publications (1974).

Notes

Notes

Notes

NOTES

Notes

Notes

www.ingramcontent.com/pod-product-compliance
Lightning Source LLC
Chambersburg PA
CBHW060537100426
42743CB00009B/1553